The Gangster Chronicles
Part One
Lucky Luciano: Architect of the Modern Mob

Frank A. Aloi
Blair T. Kenny

Illustrated by
Sam Villareale

The Gangster Chronicles
Part One
Lucky Luciano: Architect of the Modern Mob

Frank A. Aloi
Blair T. Kenny

Illustrated by
Sam Villareale

2nd edition
ISBN: 978-0-578-67895-5

Table of Contents

AUTHOR'S NOTE

This book is not intended to be a scholarly work or dissertation, but rather an anecdotal retelling of larger than life events, and the players, most colorful, few not, who shaped them. Wiseguys and law enforcement officials, State, Federal and Local, contributed their recollections. The available literature, both books and articles, was reviewed. One of the authors attended most of the trials conducted in the environs of Rochester and Buffalo, N.Y., and had access to trial transcripts and briefs. The broad outline of events and involved persons are basically true to the historic record, but the authors have at times taken the liberty to, in a sense, shape the end product to capture the rhythm and flavor of irreplaceable times and once in a lifetime 'characters', adding a pinch here and plaining down a rough edge there; certainly to enlighten, but most importantly to entertain!

Frank A. Aloi and Blair T. Kenny

DEDICATIONS:

To my parents, Laura and Tony, the best of the best, and the way it was on Scio Street in Rochester, N.Y., back in the day, with the Church of Mt. Carmel, and its School, the Aquinas Institute, playgrounds at Number 14 School, and Hartford Street, and a porch for friends and family that was the center of the world, the radio ever present, with air shots of the Big Bands and the Mel Allen era of New York Yankees broadcasts.

Frank A. Aloi

To my father, Thomas J. Kenny, who passed away in 2002. My dad was a Teamsters Business Agent in Rochester, and worked with Frank's father for many years at a local food processing plant, and with Frank himself during two summer vacations in the late '50's. When first we met a year or so ago, Frank remembered my father helping him put together a Senior paper on the Teamsters. Frank never forgot his generosity and friendship. Given the connection between our fathers, maybe it was inevitable that our 'Stars' would cross, and we would work together, as did our fathers. Here we partner as writers, and hopefully our collaborations will produce stories that readers will enjoy.

Blair T. Kenny

INTRODUCTION

The Gangster Chronicles is an overview of the American Mafia, beginning with the formation of the original Mafia "Commission", and continuing with the evolution of organized crime into all aspects of life in the modern day era. The book is presented as a four part series. Part One highlights the mafia migration, the Depression era "bootlegger/gangsters" like Lucky Luciano, Frank Costello, Al Capone, and Stephano Magaddino and others, and continues into the '40's and '50's with the mob bankrolling the Las Vegas Strip through Bugsy Siegel and Meyer Lansky; and finally into the tumultuous 1960's with the downfall of Vito Genovese, and the Coming of the Kennedys.

"The Gangster Chronicles" was literally a work in progress for decades by Frank Aloi, author of "The Hammer Conspiracies." There was a short-lived serialization of parts of the work in the '70's, and '80's, but nothing thereafter in the public domain. After his first crime book was released in 1982, Frank continued his researching and writing. Unfortunately, the rigors of a full time law practice compelled him to relegate his writing to the "back shelf".

The Gangster Chronicles project was revived following the successful collaborative work between Frank and I called "Enter The C-Team", which was released in February 2020. Shortly thereafter, I agreed to help Frank publish some of his previously unpublished work.

Frank edited "The Gangster Chronicles" text, and worked to update end notes, and bibliography. The extent of my contribution to this project involved adding illustrations, depicting major characters and events in the book, both original and historical, and the general layout and presentation of the book. For the original illustrations I enlisted local artist, Sam Villareale, who provided original art work for the Chapter intro pages and the book's cover.

With cooperative publishing improvements and a distribution network in place from my four previous books about the Rochester Mafia, I am proud to be a part of the documentation of a much larger and unique part of American history with "The Gangster Chronicles."

Blair Kenny (author of The Rochester Mob Wars) and Frank Aloi (author of The Hammer Conspiracies) being interviewed by 106.3 radio prior to the release of their book, "Enter The C-Team", The story of Thomas Taylor, Rochester Mob Associate.

Chapter 1
The Beginning:

Mussolini Comes to Power

The Beginning:
Mussolini Comes to Power

**No single ethnic group has a monopoly on crime,
organized or otherwise, but the immigrant
Sicilian Mafia is a distinct chapter of Americana.**

Turn of the Century Sicily was much as it had been for a thousand years, the present barely distinguishable from the distant past, a harshly beautiful place of fate, miracles, and superstitions; a tragic land that had bent but never broken before the armed might of countless conquerors. Romans and Greeks, Normans and Saracens, Spanish Inquisitors, the Papacy, Napoleon's legions, all tramped over the blood red dust of Sicily, and each in their turn marched into the myth that is as much Sicily, as the ruins of its oppressors.

Craggy sea cliffs stand mute before the restless roar of the Mediterranean. And on the sun drenched plains, the battlements of Norman castles stare down at the graceful marble pillars of Greek Temples, and the surreal minarets and turrets of Moslem mosques, and fortresses. All of it a breath away from destruction in the seismic trench between Mount Vesuvius in the north, and Mount Etna in the south, the island wasting in the furnace blasts of the desert sirocco that brings with it the perfumed scent of Africa just beyond the horizon.

There are olive groves, and lemon orchards, wildflowers, vineyards, and grain filled fields terraced from mountainsides, bleaching boulder strewn plains, clacking stands of bamboo, and salt mines predating Christ. In the cities, the colors of tiled roofed stucco houses proclaim their heritage, blue for the Greeks, reds and pinks for the Saracens, yellow for the Jews, and sun-bleached white for the Normans.

Mule drawn peasant carts wind their way along narrow pathways, past the medieval facades of Spanish Cathedrals, the frowning fountainheads of the Greeks gushing water from jagged mouths twisted as if in pain. Fishing fleets ply the coastal waters.

Always there are reminders that Holy Mother Church is an enduring force in Sicily. There are the brooding crucifixes, icons of worship, and instruments of death for Spartacus' vanquished slaves, resplendent Cathedrals, pastoral churches, and the ancient roadside shrines of padlocked wooden boxes sheltering statues of patron saints.

In a thousand years no one government or conqueror endured to guarantee order and earn the faith and support of the "Sicilian". Craggy faced, serious wiry men, with hooded eyes, and Arabic skin, self-reliant men, born of centuries of distrusting authority, both the governmental variety and their protected class, the landed gentry, Sicilians truly mirrored the many bloods that co-mingled in their veins. Fatalistic and melancholy, the peasantry were well aware that they, like their crops, would be harvested. Betrayed, but never beaten, these iron-willed men looked to themselves for protection from an unyielding and all too often malevolent environment.

It was in this atmosphere of turmoil and distrust, that the "mafia" was born in the 10th Century Saracen occupation. Strangely, it was not the caravan brigands who became their patron saints, but rather the great Knights Roland and Oliver who perished at the swords of the Saracen hordes because Roland in pride refused to sound his horn to summon back Charlemagne's army when a vastly superior Saracen force fell upon his rear guard.

Called the "Friends of the Friends", these men were like shadows in the morning mist rolling in from the sea, unseen, yet always there to redress grievances and sponsor and guarantee sanctuary for the oppressed. Legend and reality, however, often painted sharply differing portraits of these members of the "secret society".

With a language to disguise their intentions where information was communicated by indirection and innuendo, merciless vengeance became their rule of law, "vendetta" their religion, and "omerta", the code of silence, their anthem. Chameleon like, these "men of respect" could be "courtly" and "benevolent" sponsoring peasant sons in the great University of Palermo and underwriting the great peasant fiestas and fairs, and still be "merciless" and "unforgiving" in murdering government agents and private citizens who infringed on their territory and enterprises.

In the first decades of the 20th Century, the government in Rome resolved to bring the "Friends of the Friends" to their knees. Benito Mussolini, the shining prince of the new fascist order, declared war of the mafia, with startling and unanticipated results for America.

* * *

Benito Mussolini

On **Oct. 31, 1922**, Benito Mussolini was given the reins of government in Italy by King Victor Emmanuel III. Mussolini's rise to power had been essentially a bloodless coup. His followers had staged a massive march on Rome from each of the four points of the compass.

The government fell, and the King had no choice but to summon Mussolini, the leader of the insurgents, to restore order. Mussolini received full dictatorial powers for one year, and in that time he did in fact begin to restore order and stabilize the economy with an ambitious program of public works.

The "public" Mussolini called for a return to the splendor that was Rome, and argued that Italy's rightful Mediterranean "empire" must be restored. With large mesmerizing eyes, an ever pugnacious chin, and spellbinding rhetoric, Mussolini rallied all Italy to the call of Empire. Brandishing the Sword of Islam, the symbol of Italy's ancient conqueror, Mussolini first set his sights on Libya in North Africa, and then Abyssinia in East Africa.

But before these "holy campaigns" of conquest could begin, Mussolini knew he would first have to deal with a more imminent and pervasive problem, that of Italy's own "south". As it had for centuries, Sicily remained a thorn in the side of the government in Rome.

Within months of his inauguration, Mussolini visited Sicily, crossing the Ionian Sea from the great naval base at Taranto on the heel of the Italian "boot" on a battleship, escorted by planes above and submarines below, to enter the Straits of Messina.

The City of Messina and the surrounding countryside emptied as thousands upon thousands listened to Il Duce. Mussolini promised an end to poverty. He assured the Sicilians that he was well aware of the terrible conditions in the sulphur mines. Mussolini guaranteed that the thousands living in shanty towns and makeshift huts in the aftermath of a great earthquake 15 years before would finally be given jobs and a decent place to live. Then Mussolini declared war on the "mafia", the real reason for his visit to Messina. First and foremost, the lack of security in the countryside would be eliminated.

Mussolini was well aware that democratic institutions of government and the Courts had been manipulated for centuries by the mafia. So pervasive was their power that even journalists were intimidated, refusing to call Mafiosi by name, rather referring to them as "fugitives from justice," if at all. The new fascist order could not co-exist with the mafia shadow government in the countryside.

Too often, said Mussolini, the mafia endured by rigging local elections, and by threatening witnesses and juries. All of this, he assured, would soon end. Mussolini acted swiftly, suspending the constitutional guarantees of public trial, and instituting a nationwide round-up of suspected mafia members. More than 2,000 persons were put in prison, mainly "on suspicion," and with no presentation of evidence at trial, or otherwise.

The Sicilian mafia was crippled, but not broken. Curiously, the fascist campaign against the mafia, severe though it was, centered in eastern Sicily, rather than the west where the Friends of the Friends were really entrenched. Mountains that traversed Sicily, continuations of the Apennines of the Italian peninsula, and the Atlas of northwestern Africa, seemed to give western Sicily a kind of insular security.

The mafia still flourished in Castellammare del Golfo on the Tyrrhenian Sea, near Palermo, and further in-land, in Monreale, and Corleone. And the western port cities of Trapani and Marsala were the points of entry for ancient smuggling routes from Corsica and Sardinia, and Tunis in northwest Africa.

While fascist agents ranged through cities and countryside in search of elusive mafia bandits, the great Dons of the Mafia were convened by Don Vito Cascio Ferro to plot their course in the face of Mussolini's offensive. The occasion for the meeting of the mafia elder statesmen was the March 30, 1923 anniversary of the night of the Sicilian Vespers.

On that day in 1282, Sicilians rioted in the Church of Saint Spirito in Palermo. French soldiers had insulted local parishioners, who then took up arms and murdered the soldiers during hours of worship in the Church. The killing spread to the streets and continued through the night of March 30-31. When finally the riots subsided, more than 2,000 Frenchmen had been murdered. This moment of rage at the hour of vespers, on Easter Monday in 1282, signaled the beginning of the Sicilian revolt against the French of Charles I, which eventually would bring Peter III of Aragon to the throne.

Cascio Ferro
1902 mug shot
Born Jan.22, 1862
Died Sept. 20, 1943
(aged 81)

Don Vito Cascio Ferro feared that Mussolini's reign of terror would soon spread to western Sicily. The mass exodus of Italians to the shores of America was underway. Ellis Island was a term now familiar to these men as they dined and deliberated. Some of their number were already relocated and prospering in New York City.

There were arguments that the fascist agents would fail in their war on the secret society, as had other oppressors over hundreds of years. Yet Mussolini seemed to be striking at their heart in detaining and jailing the young men, who would be their life blood in years to come.

They argued long into the night, and finally agreed with Don Vito that their most promising sons would be sent to America to eventually set up satellite cells of the secret society. There was no time to lose. The mafia elders dispersed into the countryside to give the word of their decision to the young men who would soon be delivered to waiting ships for their voyage to America.

Chapter 2

The Mafia Migration

The Castellammarese Wars

The Mafia Migration, The Castellammarese Wars

Cesare Mori had organized the great march on Rome that ultimately brought Mussolini to power. Mussolini rewarded him with the post of Prefect of Palermo. From that prestigious office, Mori expanded the fascist purge of the mafia into the hitherto "safe" enclaves of western Sicily.

Don Vito Cascio Ferro immediately became Mori's prime target. But Don Vito would not be easily taken. For it was he who shrewdly invented the "pizzu," wetting the beak, as the modus operandi for the mafia taking its cut from the economic enterprises of the land.

Cesare Mori was born on Dec. 22, 1871 and died on July 6, 1942.

Don Vito imposed a "small tax" on virtually every economic enterprise in Sicily, preferring to "tax" moderately on a broad spectrum of goods and services, rather than impose heavy levies on a few lucrative businesses, likely to cripple them. In return, Don Vito redressed grass roots wrongs when the authorities were impervious to them.

It would not be easy for Mori to break the bonds of loyalty between the people and Don Vito. But Mori persisted with sweeps in force through cities and countryside, which eventually bagged hundreds of suspects, most of whom were tortured until they were more than willing to give the testimony desired by their captors.

Don Vito knew that it was only a matter of time before the net closed, even to his doorstep. After persuading the council of Dons to his view, Don Vito moved quickly to establish the escape route to America for the mafia's most promising young men. A great fleet of fishing boats was assembled to ferry the young Mafiosi over the first leg of the nautical journey to the new world.

Stephano Magaddino was born in Castellammare del Golfo on Oct. 10, 1891. He was the son of a mafia Don in Sicily.

The "southern route" proceeded from Sicily to Tunis, then to Cuba, and finally to the ports of entry in the Southern United States, New Orleans, Tampa, Miami, and Norfolk. The "northern route" ran from Sicily to Marseilles, and then to New York City, or into the Canadian Maritime Provinces, and thence into the United States via Buffalo, or Detroit.

Not all of the mafia young men, however, were eager to leave their homeland. Stephano Magaddino had been born in Castellammare del Golfo on Oct. 10, 1891. The son of a mafia Don, Stephano Magaddino was by his 30th year one of the "uomini di onore", the men of honor.

His family had, by virtue of an ancient "infamita", or terrible wrong, been embroiled for years in a bloody "vendetta" with the Buccillato brothers. That feud had claimed Pietro Magaddino, Stephano's brother, as its most recent victim. Stephano Magaddino spoke for brother Antonio "Nino" Magaddino, and their younger first cousin, Joseph Bonanno, in declaring an intention to remain in Sicily to avenge Pietro, despite the mounting pressure of the fascist purge.

Stephano enlisted Don Ciccio Cuccia, a colorful local leader, to plead his case with Don Vito Cascio Ferro, who had ordered the Magaddino's to leave Sicily for their own safety. It was appropriate that Stephano Magaddino chose Don Ciccio as his spokesman, since it was Don Ciccio who twice in recent history had made fools of both the King and Mussolini.

Don Ciccio had for years been Mayor of Piana dei Greci, a town located an hour's ride from Palermo. Piana dei Greci had an Albanian population, which preserved the Greek Orthodox religion as well as the language and customs of the homeland.

Years before, King Victor Emmanuel II visited Piana, and Don Ciccio put on an elaborate festa in his honor, with folk dancers, music, and native foods. In the revelry of the festa, on orders from Don Ciccio, a group of Albanian dancers separated the King from his entourage. Don Ciccio led the King into the Church where an unfamiliar Greek Orthodox ceremony was beginning. The King was led to the baptismal font, where he was handed a bawling baby. A few moments later, the priest waved his hands and the astonished King was proclaimed "godfather" to Don Ciccio's son.

During Mussolini's recent visit to Palermo, Don Ciccio rode with the Duce in an open touring car surrounded by a phalanx of fascist motorcycle troopers. Don Ciccio was upset that his "guest" required such security, and he told Mussolini, "There is no need for so many police. Your excellency has nothing to fear in this district when you are with me."

Mussolini relented and called off some of his escorts. When the touring car entered the Town Square, Don Ciccio stood up in the car and shouted, with tongue in cheek, "Let no one dare touch a hair of Mussolini's head. He is my friend and the best man in the world." Don Ciccio then delivered the Duce to a balcony where Mussolini believed he would address a throng of townspeople. To his surprise, Mussolini found himself facing an audience of twenty village idiots, one legged beggars, boot blacks, and lottery ticket sellers.

Antonino "Nino" Magaddino was born on June 18, 1897. He was Steve Magaddino's brother and Joseph Bonanno's cousin.

As wily a fox as Don Ciccio had been, Don Vito Cascio Ferro doubted that his "guile" could protect the mafia young men from the closing pincers of the fascist campaign against them. Don Vito insisted that Stephano and Nino Magaddino, and their

Antonino "Nino" Magaddino

cousin, Joseph Bonanno, leave Sicily for their own safety. Don Vito's view prevailed, and it was with reluctance that the Magaddino's and Bonanno boarded a fishing boat for passage to Marseilles, and thence New York City.

Joseph Bonanno was a first cousin to the Magaddino brothers.

The final leg of their passage into the United States began in Havana and took the Magaddino's and Bonanno to New York City, and via the St. Lawrence, to Buffalo. There in late 1924, they became a part of an already burgeoning colony of Castellammarese emigrees in Brooklyn.

Carlo Gambino had preceded them on Dec. 23, 1921, and Joe Profaci, Joe Maglioco, and Mike Coppola followed in 1926, with Salvatore Maranzano entering in 1927. By virtue of his Sicilian pedigree, Stephano Magaddino quickly assumed a position of trust and responsibility in the Brooklyn Castellammarese community. But the vendetta he had left behind in Sicily all too soon caught up with him.

Stephano Magaddino, and pal Gaspar Milazzo, were walking out of a store in Brooklyn when an assassin opened fire on them. Neither man was hit, but the ambush took the lives of two innocent bystanders. The Buccillato clan had followed the Magaddino's to New York.

Gasper Milazzo

Stephano Magaddino's response was swift, and final. In the face of unredressed ancient wrongs, and this most recent attempt on his life, merciless vengeance was the only possible course. Three members of the Buccillato clan were killed, two in New York, one in New Jersey.

The New York killings caused scarcely a ripple, but an arrest warrant was issued for Magaddino in New Jersey. Rather than deal with the police, Magaddino left New York City and resettled in Buffalo, where he would remain until his death some 50 years later. It was literally from the front stoop of his family home in Lewiston that Magaddino became the "indisputable lord paramount" of the organization in western New York, and one of the original nine members of the "la costa nostra" National Commission.

From his first days in Buffalo, to the end of his life in the 70's, Stephano Magaddino established himself as a low profiled "man of respect". Magaddino was scarcely in place on the Niagara Frontier when he was drawn into the "politics" of power in the Brooklyn Castellammarese community.

First, a mobster named Mimi attempted to shakedown a "still" operated by Joe Bonanno. Bonanno resisted, and threatened to kill Mimi. Since Mimi too had backers in the Sicilian community, a hearing was convened before Vito Bonventre, a community leader.

Stephano Magaddino traveled to New York from Buffalo to act as "counsel" for his cousin, Joseph Bonanno. A rustic, deliberate man, intelligent but not outgoing, short and powerfully built, Magaddino wore his old country roots in his appearance and manners. He was, in a sense, "royalty", and his very presence as Bonanno's defender should have been enough to settle the controversy in his favor.

But Salvatore Maranzano, too, put in an unanticipated appearance on Bonanno's behalf. The absolute antithesis of Magaddino, Maranzano was ever the patrician in demeanor. Whether quoting the classics or Julius Ceasar, Maranzano was as formidable in a "drawing room" sense as Magaddino would have been in the countryside.

The defense of Joseph Bonanno was, for Stephano Magaddino, purely and simply a matter of family. Bonanno was of the same blood, and Magaddino would defend him regardless of the consequences.

Salvatore Maranzano (July 31, 1886 - Sept. 10, 1931)

Salvatore Maranzano's intervention was quite another matter. Maranzano shrewdly discerned in the youthful Bonanno a potential for leadership, and an ambition, which could fit nicely with Maranzano's own designs for criminal grandeur. Bonanno was, of course, exonerated. But Stephano Magaddino returned to Buffalo feeling somewhat badly used, and wondering just where his cousin's ambitions would take him, and at whose expense.

A homebody who shunned the public spotlight, and night life, Stephano Magaddino literally "stayed home" while his flamboyant brother, Antonio "Nino"'Magaddino, attended early mob conventions in his stead, the first called by Joe Profaci at a Cleveland hotel in **December of 1928**, the second hosted by Frank Costello and "Nucks" Johnson in May of 1929 in Atlantic City. To the locals, "Nino" was the Don, the man out front who did the gambling spots and night clubs, and brother Stephano did nothing to dispel the notion.

On Dec. 5, 1928, Joe Porrello and his lieutenant and bodyguard Sam Tilocco hosted the first known major meeting of the Mafia at Cleveland's Hotel Statler.

Many major Mafia leaders from Chicago to New York to Florida were invited. The meeting was raided before it actually began. Joe Profaci, leader of a Brooklyn, N.Y. Mafia family was the most well-known of the gangsters arrested. He was the founder of the Colombo Mafia family. Vincent Mangano also ranked high as founder of the Gambino family . " – *AmericanMafia.com*

Prohibition was a bonanza for Magaddino, since Buffalo sat astride the most direct smuggling route down the St. Lawrence and across Lake Erie, or Ontario, from the Canadian distilleries. Gambling rooms and speakeasies flourished, as did the lottery and mob shylocking. Many businesses paid for dubious "protection". Immigration, the illegal variety, likewise padded the mob's coffers. So, too, did infiltration into legitimate businesses including a taxi company and linen supply, restaurants, and liquor distributorships. Overtures were also made to early trade unions. These "interests" were most often fronted for Magaddino by his "compare", and underboss, John C. Montana. It would take the catastrophic mob convention at Apalachin some 30 years later to unmask the civic minded "businessman" John C. Montana as a close associate of mafia Don, Stephano Magaddino.

Joe Masseria, mugshot by the New York Police Department

Business was indeed "good" for the Magaddino "family" in Western New York, but the Castellammarese pot began to boil in Brooklyn in a vicious gang war that would require every mafiosi to declare "sides". Joe "the Boss" Masseria* was the entrenched mob boss of Brooklyn, with tentacles reaching into the remainder of New York City and New Jersey. Salvatore Maranzano, and a splinter group of Castellammarese, had designs on the "empire" of Joe the Boss, and soon shakedowns and street shootings became the order of the day as Masseria resisted the Maranzano takeover.

Maranzano called on fellow Castellammarese, Magaddino, to back his play. Magaddino did so at the cost of "soldiers" and supplies loaned to Maranzano, and some $5,000 each week contributed to Maranzano's war "treasury". For a time, it looked as if Joe the Boss would prevail by sheer weight of numbers. He enlisted a powerful ally in Al Capone in Chicago by a curious but telling ploy.

Unlike Maranzano and Magaddino, neither Joe "the Boss" Masseria, nor his principal allies, were pedigreed Sicilian mafiosi. Masseria perceived that Capone resented the old worldly, stand offish, courtly mafia Dons, the "mustache pete's", as he called them. Not only did Masseria back Capone with men and money in his Chicago war with "Bugs" Moran and Joe Aiello, but also Masseria promised to install Capone as the "Don" of a new Chicago mafia "family" when the war was won.

---

*Joe Masseria (Jan. 17, 1886 – April 15, 1931) was an early Italian-American Mafia boss in New York City. He was boss of what is now called the Genovese crime family, one of the New York City Mafia's Five Families, from 1922 to 1931. In 1930, he battled in the Castellammarese War to take over the criminal activities in New York City. The war ended with his murder on April 15, 1931 in a hit ordered by his own lieutenant, Charles "Lucky" Luciano, in an agreement with rival faction head, Salvatore Maranzano.

Al Capone
Chicago Mob Boss

By early **1929**, Al Capone was on the offensive, and on **Feb. 14**, he put his personal "signature" on the slaughter of Bugs Moran's boys that would forever more be known as the St. Valentine's Day Massacre. Of course, Masseria himself was not of the right blood or background to deliver his promised mafia imprimatur for Capone, but this somehow became lost in the shuffle as the gang war approached its critical point.

On Feb. 14, 1929, seven men associated with the Irish gangster, George "Bugs" Moran, Capone's longtime enemy, were shot to death by several men dressed as policemen. The St. Valentine's Day Massacre, as it was known, was never officially linked to Capone.

There was "stalemate" for a time in New York City, as both sides jockeyed for position. Independent gangsters were courted. Dutch Schultz in Harlem and the Bronx elected to remain neutral. But Lucky Luciano in Brooklyn was quite another matter. Like Capone, Luciano, while Sicilian, was not of mafia blood. Masseria passed the word that he was meeting with Luciano and made Luciano the same proposition he had made to Capone, men, money, and pedigree as a Mafia Don. Luciano knew that mafia status was not to be achieved by Masseria's decree, yet Joe the Boss seemed to be winning, and Luciano loved to back a "winner."

Chapter 3
Luciano's Luck,

Maranzano's Misfortune

Luciano's Luck, Maranzano's Misfortune

By the **beginning of 1930**, the forces of Joe "the Boss" Masseria had gained the upper hand. Gaspar Milazzo, a close friend of Stephano Magaddino, was boss of Detroit's mafia family, and following Magaddino's lead, he had allied himself with fellow Castellammarese, Salvatore Maranzano. Magaddino urged Milazzo to keep a low profile, but Gaspar Milazzo stubbornly stayed public.

In **early 1930**, Masseria's "soldiers" caught up with Milazzo, killing him in a Detroit fishmarket. In the aftermath of Milazzo's assassination, Joe Aiello retreated from his Chicago "war" with Al Capone that was going badly, and sought sanctuary with Stephano Magaddino in Buffalo.

Charles "Lucky"
Luciano
Nov. 24, 1897 –
Jan. 26, 1962

As one of the "senior" Castellammarese "Dons" operating in the new world, Magaddino was a "patrone" or "head man" for his kinsmen, wherever they were located. Magaddino left the actual New York City fighting to Salvatore Maranzano, but continued to back Maranzano with money, men, and material.

Joe "the Boss" Masseria realized that while Maranzano was the cutting edge for the Castellammarese, Magaddino, with his Sicilian mafia roots, gave them legitimacy, even in America. Masseria resolved to eliminate Magaddino, by luring him to New York City for a peace parlay. Magaddino was not so easily deceived, and he ignored Masseria's alternating pleas and threats for a meeting.

Joe Aiello was killed when Capone gunmen ambushed him as he exited a Chicago apartment building where he had been hiding out. He was shot 59 times.

Joe Aiello was less shrewd. Al Capone sent word to Buffalo that he wanted to settle his differences with Aiello. Magaddino smelled a trap, but Aiello decided nonetheless to meet with Capone. Capone never showed, but a car load of his killers did, and Aiello was murdered.

Masseria had himself been in hiding, but in an incredible stroke of good fortune, he was located. Maranzano henchman, Joe Valachi, had staked out an apartment building in the Bronx rented by Masseria's "soldiers." Masseria showed up, and Valachi, with reinforcements, closed in for the kill. The ambush "net" remained around the building for days. Still, Masseria was not sighted leaving the building.

It finally seemed that Joe the Boss must have given them the slip. Just as Valachi's hit team was about to disperse, a group of men broke from the building. In the ensuing shootout, Al Mineo and Steve Ferrigno, two close Masseria cronies, were killed, but not "Joe the Boss." Valachi searched the building, but Masseria had again slipped the noose. Everything seemed to be going Masseria's way.

Joe Valachi

The charismatic Maranzano knew that things were going badly. By this time, the canny Lucky Luciano, smelling the tide turning for Joe the Boss Masseria, had become Masseria's underboss. That meant the defection too of Luciano's inner cadre, the cerebral Meyer Lansky, the diplomatic Frank Costello, and the lethal Bugsy Siegel.

Maranzano consulted with Stephano Magaddino and the two Castellammarese leaders hit upon the strategy of "turning" Lucky Luciano, and through Charlie Lucky, getting rid of Masseria. Magaddino met with Luciano.

The liquor smuggling routes to Long Island Sound and the Jersey shore were open to attack by the Prohibition agents and the Coast Guard. Luciano was looking for "points" in a safer smuggling route. Magaddino's "empire" sat astride just such a route across the Great Lakes from Canada. Luciano perceived Magaddino as a man he could do business with, but deferred striking the deal to mull it over with his boys. Magaddino saw that Charlie Lucky was hooked, and didn't press for a commitment.

Maranzano was incensed when he learned that Luciano had left the meeting still technically allied with "Joe the Boss" Masseria. Maranzano met with Luciano and asked his allegiance. Still, Luciano deferred, saying the time wasn't right, and that he'd let Maranzano know when the "deal" could be done. Maranzano felt he was being toyed with. In a rage, he "arranged" another "meet" with Charlie Lucky.

This time Luciano was blindfolded and strung up by his thumbs on an isolated Staten Island dock. Charlie Lucky absorbed a terrible beating, but remained silent. Maranzano finally broke cover, and asked Luciano why he persisted in stubbornly refusing to take the "deal." Luciano said nothing. A Maranzano henchman brandished a stiletto and slashed Luciano's face.

Charlie Lucky would carry the scar and the memory of his nocturnal meeting with Maranzano for the rest of his days. Unconscious, and bleeding, Luciano was cut down. Maranzano drove off, feeling that even a hard case like Luciano would come around after such an "object lesson."

Luciano survived, and kept an unnerving silence about the incident. Outwardly, he remained Joe the Boss Masseria's underboss, meeting with him, and looking to the business side of Masseria's empire. Finally, Luciano contacted Magaddino, and alerted him that the time was near. Stephano Magaddino passed the word to Salvatore Maranzano, who smiled smugly in the knowledge that his harsh "medicine" had finally taken to "persuade" Luciano to come around.

**Joe "the Boss"
Masseria's
last game of cards.**

On **April 15, 1931**, Lucky Luciano met Joe "the Boss" Masseria for lunch at the Nuova Villa Tammaro on Coney Island. After lunch, the two men played cards. An hour into the game, Luciano excused himself to visit the men's room.

Bugsy Siegel walked into the restaurant, moved directly to Masseria's table, and fired four shots into the head and chest of Joe the Boss. The mob gave Joe the Boss a regal send-off in a solid silver coffin. There were 69 cars in the funeral procession, including 16 filled with flowers.

With Joe the Boss out of the way, Salvatore Maranzano now had a clear field to the goal he craved, his "coronation" as boss of all bosses. There did remain one stumbling block, Al Capone in Chicago. Maranzano toyed with taking the war to the Chicago boss and putting him "under," once and for all. Stephano Magaddino argued Maranzano out of that strategy and persuaded him instead to appeal to Capone's "vanity" with diplomacy.

Magaddino understood that Capone dearly wanted to be designated "father" or "Don" of a new Chicago mafia family. He suggested that Maranzano not only bestow that "honor" on Capone but also journey to Chicago to do it. This would surely "disarm" Capone and also give Maranzano the opportunity to preside over his own coronation as national boss.

The arrangements were made, and Maranzano boarded a train in New York City for Chicago. With him were new underboss Lucky Luciano, and recent protege, Joe Bonanno. The train stopped in Buffalo where Stephano Magaddino, and his right hand man, John C. Montana, boarded.

Maranzano quoted the classics and waxed eloquent about the manifest destiny of his forthcoming coronation. Magaddino deferred to Maranzano and rather used the tedium of the train ride to discuss "business" with Lucky Luciano. There was a curious chemistry between Magaddino, the old world mafiosi, and Luciano, the upstart mob boss from "hell's kitchen", that wasn't lost on Salvatore Maranzano.

Al Capone literally turned the City of Chicago out for the mob convention at the Hotel Congress. Capone footed the bill for the opulent mob bash, even sending Maranzano a gold watch studded with diamonds. Maranzano was guest of honor at a climactic banquet. After glowing introductions for the assembled "dignitaries," Maranzano rose to address them.

First, he recounted the "heroic" annals of the Castellammarese war, so recently concluded over the dead body of Joe "the Boss" Masseria. He designated mob bosses for the various New York City territories and other cities now under his jurisdiction, Chicago, Detroit, Cleveland, Buffalo, and the rest.

Maranzano spoke of loyalty, and respect, but mostly he advised his assembled Dons of his absolute certainty that it was his fate to lead them. Maranzano spoke glowingly of the "glory" he would bring to all of them. Stephano Magaddino knew it came down to blood, money, and guns, but this was Maranzano's moment, and he'd do nothing to cloud it.

Lucky Luciano stood at Maranzano's right hand, his new underboss. The evening closed with each of "Ceasar's" subjects handing Maranzano an envelope stuffed with money. Maranzano left the Hotel Congress that night several hundred thousand dollars richer.

Stephano Magaddino was not yet 40, but with his "impeccable" Sicilian roots, he was already the Senior Catellmmarese mafia Don, and a person whose "approval" could lend an air of legitimacy to any venture. He returned home from Chicago uneasy with Maranzano's delusions of grandeur, but resolved to wait and see what might develop.

Maranzano had spoken of "ruling" the criminal empire only in consultation with his senior bosses, but as the months dragged on, it became apparent that Maranzano "governed" in much the same

Vincent "Mad Dog" Coll was hired by Joe Masseri to kill Lucky Luciano

way as had the Roman Emperors he so admired, "absolutely," and without questions.

Stephano Magaddino knew that an explosion would not be long in coming, but still he resolved not to be its instigator. In the late **summer of 1931**, Lucky Luciano secretly met with Magaddino. Luciano told him that Maranzano had hired Vincent "Mad Dog" Coll to kill him. Luciano intended to defend himself, even if that meant striking first at Maranzano.

Magaddino, his partner in the Canadian and Great Lakes smuggling routes, would not interfere in what he deemed an intrafamily dispute between Maranzano and his underboss. Magaddino did, however, suggest to Luciano that perhaps Dutch Schultz, Vincent Coll's sometime boss, and an independent gangster working in Luciano's territory, might get to Coll and persuade him to call off the "contract." Luciano promised to try Schultz first, before taking matters into his own hands, and the meeting ended on that note.

Luciano did in fact parlay with Schultz, but the erstwhile "Dutchman" demurred, explaining that not even he could rein in Coll when the "Mad Dog" had accepted blood money. Lucky Luciano had his doubts about Schultz' motives, but that would have to wait until he took care of Maranzano's contract.

Vito Genovese volunteered to "hit" Maranzano, but Luciano decided against using the serpentine Genovese. Maranzano would be watching him, even expecting it from that quarter. Rather, Luciano again gave the "hard contract" to Bugsy Siegel, admonishing him that there was no time to lose.

Swift, violent inspiration was Siegel's forte. Siegel quickly devised the way in, literally, to Maranzano's office. Maranzano was being audited by the IRS. Tax agents were camped daily at this office. Siegel's crew would appear as "Revenue Agents" and march right into Maranzano's outer office, to do him in.

On Sept. 10, 1931 Lucky Luciano's hitman entered Maranzano's office building on the 9th floor of The Helmsley Building, posing as tax men to raid the building. Maranzano's guards were dis- armed, and fled the scene (including Mad Dog Coll who was about to sit in a meeting with Maranzano).

On **Sept. 10, 1931,** Siegel and three henchmen appeared in Maranzano's office in the Grand Central Building at 46th Street and Park Avenue. The quartet flashed 'ID' and were led up the stairs to Maranzano's personal office. Maranzano's bodyguards were easily disarmed. Maranzano, misperceiving their intentions, himself led Siegel's men to his inner office. There, Siegel and company made short work of Salvatore Maranzano. The "boss of bosses" was stabbed and shot four times.

As Maranzano drew his last breath, Siegel and his crew vaulted down the stairs to the street. As they reached the street, Vinnie Coll passed them going the other way, presumably to get final instructions on the "Luciano hit." Siegel shouted to Coll "The guy you work for just had an attack." Taking that to mean that Maranzano was dead, Coll did an about face and left the building. Without Maranzano there would be no hit on Luciano. Nor would there by any refund.

In the aftermath of Salvatore Maranzano's death, a mob realignment was inevitable. Some 60 Maranzano loyalists were purged across the country in an episode now christened "the night of the Sicilian vespers." It didn't happen in a "night" nor did it have anything to do with Sicilian history. Charlie Lucky was simply clearing the decks for the resumption of mob business in an "orderly" fashion."

Bugsy Siegel was given the contracts to kill both Mob Bosses, Maranzanno and Masseria. He was also one of the shooters.

As the architect of the "double cross" that had removed both "Joe the Boss" Masseria, and Salvatore Maranzano, Lucky Luciano was now expected to call the tune as to how the organization functioned in the coming years.

Most of the "soldiers" expected another "coronation" and for Luciano to function in much the same way as had his predecessor. Charlie Lucky, however, was never one to make the expected play. There was major mob business at hand, with enormous profits to be made. The mob was infiltrating the garment district. The beginnings of expansion to the west was on the agenda, as was the mob's most lucrative post-prohibition endeavor, narcotics smuggling.

Before declaring his intentions for the national organization, Luciano first attended to some internal housekeeping. With Maranzano dead, his New York "family" was without a "head." The youthful Joe Bonanno was Luciano's choice to take over, and no

Joe Bonanno

voice was raised against him. Next, Luciano returned to Chicago and again convened the heads of the New York families, and those in New Jersey, Chicago, and Buffalo.

* * *

Original Mafia Commission 1931

The 1st Mafia Commission in 1931.

It was Luciano's idea that these men function as a "national commission," governing major policy aspects of mob business. In the event of a deadlock, Luciano himself would cast the deciding vote. As originally conceived, the mob commission was an eight man thing, the five New York families, New Jersey, Buffalo, and Chicago.

At various times thereafter, its composition was expanded to include a representative from Detroit, Philadelphia, and New England. Luciano proposed that old pals Meyer Lansky and Bugsy Siegel handle the "enforcement" end of the mob's business. The old "Bug and Meyer" gang, however, had other things in mind. First with Hollywood, then Las Vegas, and finally the Bahamas and Havana; over a 20 year period they would, with Luciano's blessing, expand considerably the mob's gambling and resort business.

Albert Anastasia

Quickly, the job of enforcing commission decrees fell to Lepke Buchalter, who eventually teamed with Albert Anastasia to found the infamous "Murder, Inc.," the mob's murder for profit business.

Lepke Buchalter

Chapter 4
The Cops, The Crooks,
and the Big Rich

Chicago, After Capone

The Cops, The Crooks, and the Big Rich
Chicago, After Capone

The mandate of the Federal Grand Jury probing the taxes of one Alphonse Capone was to expire on March 15, 1931. After that date, the Statute of Limitations would bar IRS investigators from opening some of the years for which Capone was believed to *be* most vulnerable. As the Ides of March approached, each day passing without word from the Grand Jury, many in Chicago believed that Al Capone had indeed dodged another bullet, finally "prevailing" upon the Government to accept his offer in settlement for all tax arrears, an amount rumored to exceed $1,500,000. But on March 13, 1931, there was word from the Grand Jury that an indictment had been returned against Chicago's most notorious citizen.

The indictment would be sealed until the Grand Jury completed its probe of the tax years 1925 thru 1929, but that was small comfort for Capone. Only four years earlier, several of his closest cronies, including Frank 'the Enforcer' Nitti and Jake 'Greasy Thumb' Guzik, had been charged, convicted and jailed in tax fraud cases. For "the big fella", the handwriting was clearly on the wall. His lawyers could buy him time, but in the not too distant future 'Uncle Sam' would finally have its way with the Chicago gangster, setting in motion the prosecution that would

eventually put him behind bars. By the end of **October 1931**, Al Capone had begun serving an 11 year sentence at the Federal Penitentiary in Atlanta.

The times indeed were changing in the "Windy City". The St. Valentine's Day massacre in 1929 had put to rest once and forever any sentiment that Al Capone was a "prohibition robin hood" and persecuted "folk hero", all of his public posturing, and token works of philanthropy, soup kitchens, Holiday turkeys and contributions to the Diocese, to the contrary notwithstanding.

No longer did Capone receive "good press" from Chicago's ace crime reporter, Jake Lingle. Lingle had from day one been Capone's creation. His friendship with the "big fella" was legend. Capone sealed it with a diamond studded belt buckle, cash pay offs, and illegal stock market tips that made Lingle a very wealthy man.

Unaccountably, Lingle began believing that it was he, and not Capone, who ran the town. At one point Lingle bragged, "I fixed the price of beer in this town." Then Jake accepted $60,000 from Capone in return for Lingle using his influence at City Hall to gain approval for a dog track operation backed by Capone. Lingle swallowed the money and failed to deliver the approval.

Jake Lingle,
Chicago's ace crime reporter.

Jake was walking in a subway underpass on Michigan Avenue when Al Capone settled his account. A passerby came up behind Jake and put one slug into the base of his skull. Capone lamented the passing of his "dear friend" Jake. Murdering a reporter was unheard of, even in prohibition Chicago. But slowly "the real" Jake Lingle emerged in the editorials, and Chicago understood that Jake was just another hired hand of "the big fella," who had strayed and paid the price.

With Al Capone spending more and more time at this Florida estate, and returning to Chicago only to answer the charges being generated by Elliot Ness, his 28 year old T-man nemesis, and the IRS, the day to day control of the Chicago rackets gradually passed to Frank Nitti, who had "replaced" the boss in Suite 654 of the Wacker-La Salle Building, the unofficial headquarters of the underworld in Chicago, and all of it with Capone's "blessing"!

If the political status quo could be preserved, and that meant the re-election of William Hale "Big Bill" Thompson, Chicago's three time Mayor, there was the reasonable probability that it would be business as usual for the Chicago outfit, even in Capone's absence. Thompson's opponent was Anton Cermak, who had graduated from Cicero politics to become a ward leader, alderman, and finally council member in Chicago.

Cermak had been friendly enough to "the big fella" in his Cicero days, earning the nickname "10% Tony", but in 1931, Cermak was making noises about real reform, and the Capone crowd early on decided not to gamble on him and to again throw their money and ward healers behind Big Bill Thompson's re-election bid.

1931 Chicago approached the new year as would a becalmed schooner drifting through the doldrums into the black and purple skies of a terrible storm just beyond the horizon. Everyone wanted to believe that the "great depression" was the creation of the bankers of New York City, and would spend itself in the east. But "hard times" were already upon the "Windy City".

Shanty towns of the homeless and destitute were springing up - "Hoovervilles", in plain view of "The Loop". "Nice people" still met under the clock at Marshal Field & Company, while "the notorious" found the lobby of the Sherman House more to their liking. Barney Ross was the fighting pride of Chicago. Red Grange still carried the mail for the Bears, and now Bronco Nagurski had joined him, and the Cubs were still solid at Wrigley Field. But the "handwriting" was already on the wall, and in the strangest of places.

From "time immemorial" in Chicago, the "New Year" was ushered in at Bathhouse John Coughlin's First Ward Ball, held annually in the cavernous Coliseum. On the very spot where William Jennings Bryan made his "Cross of Gold" speech, Bathhouse John and his partner in crime, Hinky Dink Kenna, hosted their bacchanal where blue bloods mingled with the dregs of the underworld, saints and sinners, pimps and bank presidents, bootleggers and policemen, gangsters and politicians, whores and socialites, on this single night united in their "classless" worship of every imaginable carnal pleasure, and excess.

But **1931** was not a year like prior years. Where in years past 25,000 revelers had packed the coliseum shoulder to shoulder, this year saw a meager 2,000 attend. The great City's clock was slowing. In time its "batteries" would recharge, but as 1931 became myth and memory, there was the "feeling" that the "smart money" would expect the unexpected.

Bombastic "Big Bill" Thompson was a known quantity. Chicago's mainliners had come to terms with Thompson, and helped re-elect him three times. Anton Cermak was Chicago's first "foreign" mayoral candidate. Cermak was Slavic. Would the middle Europeans, Slavs, Poles and Germans unite to cast their ballots for "10% Tony"? If they did, and Chicago's old line 'big rich' threw in with them, Cermak would win hands down, regardless of the conviction of Capone and his underworld crowd that "Big Bill" Thompson was still good for business.

The banking and business community in 1932 Chicago was by and large the creation of two men, General Charles Gates Dawes and Samuel Insull. General Dawes had served with "Black Jack" Pershing in the Great War, albeit not in the field, but as the U.S. Army "purchasing agent". After the war it was Dawes who formulated the plan for the reconstruction of post-war Europe.

Dawes became the first director of the newly created Bureau of the Budget under President Harding, and was a valued member of Harding's "Poker Cabinet". Never simply a one dimensional "money man", Dawes was an accomplished musician who wrote a short piece for violin called "Melody in A Major" that was quite popular in its day. That melody was revived in the 50's as the pop song hit, "It's All in the Game."

When Harding died in office, General Dawes agreed to run as the vice presidential running mate for Calvin Coolidge, and it was Dawes who actually stumped the country for the "withdrawn" Coolidge. After Coolidge's term, his successor, Herbert Hoover, named Dawes to head of the Reconstruction Finance Corporation, Hoover's device for dealing with the increasing number of business failures in the widening depression.

Dawes' government service did not prevent him from building and serving as the president of the largest bank in Chicago. And as the number of displaced and homeless increased in the economic "hard times", Dawes founded a number of hostels for homeless men. But there was always a touch of Chicago in General Charles Gates Dawes. Three weeks after General Dawes resigned his position as the head of the Reconstruction Finance Corporation, the RFC loaned him 90 million dollars to save his bank.

Sam Insull was born in Victorian England, and took his first major job as assistant to the European representative for Thomas Alva Edison. Insull graduated from that job to become Edison's personal secretary in New Jersey. There, Insull became the valet, business secretary, and personal friend of Edison in his most creative years of invention.

It was Insull who put together the first of Edison's giant corporations, the Edison General Electric Corporation, eventually "GE", and it was Insull who preserved for Edison a $5,000,000 buyout when J. P. Morgan and other New York City corporate raiders took over GE from the Edison people. Insull turned down Morgan's offer to stay on in an executive capacity with the New York "GE", and opted for personal empire building, first with Chicago General Electric, and later with the giant Insull Utility Holding Company.

Insull built a billion dollar financial empire with his innovative creation of the modern system of gas and electric utilities, based on local monopolies. And it was Insull who was able to beat back the repeated attempts of J.P. Morgan, and his crony Cyrus Eaton, to take over his empire, by the then novel device of doing public stock offerings to raise the necessary capital to keep vital blocks of stock out of the "raiders" hands.

Insull presided over his multi-state empire from his 4,000 acre estate at Libertyville, Illinois. But for the great depression, Insull's reign atop his 'utility' empire would have been long indeed. But the seemingly bottomless economic downturn of the late twenties forced Insull to resort to desperate expedients to prop up the value of his stock, and beat back yet another attempt by the New York robber barons to seize control of his holdings.

In 1930, Insull borrowed $48,000,000, half of it from New York City banks to buy out the holdings of Cyrus Eaton, Morgan's partner, in Insull Securities. From that time on, Insull waged a desperate struggle with Morgan and company to stave off a personal "armageddon", as the ever resourceful J.P. Morgan repeatedly attempted to break the market in Insull's stock.

Sam Insull's struggle with the New York City bankers placed the very pillars of the Chicago financial community in jeopardy. General Dawes, and a number of other influential Chicago bankers, had invested heavily in Insull securities. If Insull went down, so too would the entire Chicago banking community. Worse, the Arch Diocese of Chicago, another substantial Insull investor, would be in jeopardy of financial ruin if the New York bankers succeeded in breaking the market in Sam Insull's stock.

Without the knowledge of Dawes, or most of the other Chicago institutional investors in Insull securities, Sam Insull hit upon a desperation tactic that for a time did shore up his crumbling financial empire. Through Sam Ettelson, the City of Chicago Corporation Counsel, and Insull's "man", and Mayor Thompson himself, Insull arranged for the interest free deposit of millions of dollars of City of Chicago money in his investor banks, whose Presidents quickly got the "message" to use those funds to buy more Insull stock and in so doing drive up the price of the stock, and break the New York City "bear" raid on the stock.

It was a tactic that couldn't miss for the banks, provided their Insull stock continued to rise. At a point the banks could sell off some of the Insull stock at increased prices and use the profits to pay back the City of Chicago deposits, maybe even at "interest" that hadn't been part of the deal. However, if Insull's stock became worthless, the City money would be lost; and not only would the banks fail, but also, their officers who had mis-used City funds on deposit would face indictment and jail terms. All that stood between the "big rich" and their undoing should Insull's empire crash was none other than "Big Bill" Thompson, the mayor suddenly in jeopardy of failing in his bid for re-election, and who just happened to be the only person who knew specifically who had received the huge City deposits.

Thompson's "discretion" could, of course, be relied on in return for certain economic considerations of the "cash" variety. But even that would be of no value if Cermak took the office and made good on his promise to clean up the town.

All the political plotting was to no avail, as Anton Cermak literally destroyed "Big Bill" Thompson at the polls by the astounding plurality of 194,267 votes. At City Hall there was a furious rush of activity prior to Cermak's inauguration as Thompson personally orchestrated the destruction of account records and the fabrication of "financial tracks" that would make difficult, if not impossible, the eventual location by Cermak's men and of the millions in City funds that had been placed in interest free deposits with the Chicago banks, to quickly be transformed by desperate bank presidents into thou-sands of shares of stock in Sam Insull's rapidly sinking utility empire.

The Spring of 1932 held another "call" date for Insull on a number of notes held by New York City lenders, to the tune of more than $10,000,000. Without another injection of interest free City money, Insull was unlikely to weather this crisis, and the whole "house of cards" would come tumbling down around the "blue bloods" of Chicago who had bet on Insull, and lost.

Chapter 5

10% Tony

10% Tony

Anton Cermak

Anton Cermak defeated Bill Thompson, becoming Chicago's new mayor. He targeted Al Capone's operations and shook them down.

The Chicago outfit would certainly have preferred another victory by "Big Bill" Thompson, if for no other reason than that he was a "known" quantity. But there was some hope that Anton Cermak would remember his gravy days in Cicero, and decide to "play ball" with the outfit once the public posturing of reform had gone on long enough to satisfy the change minded electorate that had placed him in office. Anton Cermak, however, had his own ideas about who would run the Chicago underworld in the absence of Al Capone.

Cermak's reform movement was not targeted against crime and criminals generally, but rather only against the operations of Al Capone. It quickly become apparent that it would be business as usual in Chicago, but with Cermak running the Capone outfit through his handpicked "captain", Roger Touhy, a bootlegger in the northwest suburbs.

As a signal that he meant business, Cermak ordered a concerted series of raids on Capone's speakeasies, and gambling rooms, as well as his prostitute "cribs". Frank Nitti protested and met secretly with Cermak. The Mayor would not back down and demanded of Nitti twice the "juice" in weekly payments as the price of peace. Nitti refused, and Cermak countered with a proposal pursuant to which Nitti would cede half the beer distributorships in and about Chicago to the Roger Touhy gang. Again, Frank Nitti said "no dice", and Chicago slipped into an uneasy quiet as the aggressive Mayor and stubborn gangster circled each other, looking for the opening that would take the other down.

Perhaps because there was a lull in his war of nerves with the Chicago "outfit", Cermak finally turned with a vengeance to the question of the missing City of Chicago deposits. By that time Sam Insull's empire was in ruin. Petitions in Bankruptcy had been filed, and there was no likelihood in the immediate future that Insull's stock would ever regain a significant amount of its former value. Insull's downfall seemed to trigger Cermak's determination to find the missing City money.

It took months to reconstruct the records that "Big Bill" Thompson had dutifully destroyed; but gradually, the Cermak people began to get the picture, and the ever resourceful Mayor began meeting with the offending bankers, offering them a "bargain with the devil" choice - either immediately restore the deposits with interest, an expedient now impossible, in the aftermath of Insull's bankruptcy; or begin making "cash" contributions to Anton Cermak's newly constituted political machine, payoffs that would continue indefinitely and would be the only insurance that the 'blue bloods' could look to against prosecution for their defalcation of the City funds.

It seemed as if Mayor Anton Cermak had "the trump" on both the "crooks" and "the big rich" in Chicago. Then, unaccountably, when Cermak seemed to have the Capone "outfit" on the ropes, he decided to apply a "knock out" blow that would settle once and for all who ran the Windy city. It was a step too far, and unnecessary in any event, but Cermak could not be talked out of it by advisers as greedy, but more cautious.

Frank Nitti

It had become routine for members of Cermak's private police force to visit Frank Nitti's office on the fifth floor of the Wacker-La Salle Building. They usually came in pairs, and Nitti's bodyguards became accustomed to admitting them.

On **Dec. 19, 1932,** police sergeants Harry Lang and Harry Miller, Mayor Cermak's most trusted enforcers, were ordered by "his honor" to pay Frank Nitti a visit, and "Christmas greetings" were not part of their instructions.

The pair of "detectives" flashed their tin and breezed past Louis "Little New York" Campagna and four bookmakers in Nitti's outer office. "Little New York" was Frank Nitti's bodyguard and closest associate, but Nitti had instructed him to make no waves when Cermak's boys came calling. It was a war of nerves, but Nitti had resolved to do nothing that would give the new Mayor any excuse to shut him down.

Nitti knew the detectives and ushered them into his private office. Nitti offered them cigars when they dropped into the chairs before his desk. They wasted no time advising Frank Nitti that they had orders to take him in. Nitti was puzzled, but still he offered no resistance as the detectives "invited" him to come out from behind his desk to take the ride downtown. Nitti moved around his desk and then without warning the detectives pounced on him and began wrestling his arms behind him for cuffing. Nitti screamed that the rough stuff wasn't necessary, but the detectives kept at it.

In the next instant one of them screamed, "He's got a gun," and both pulled their weapons and began blasting away at Nitti. The mob boss was hit in the back, chest and neck, and as he slumped to the floor, Louie "Little New York" Campagna stormed in and was pistol whipped by Cermak's flying squad. In minutes, Nitti's office was swarming with ambulance people and a back up squad of detectives. A gun was found under Nitti's body, and identified by the detectives as the piece Nitti had pulled on them that had begun the shoot out.

Frank Nitti was bundled onto a gurney and rushed to a hospital. He was unconscious and not expected to live. The Chicago papers speculated as to what had set off the usually cool headed Nitti to pull a gun in the face of nothing more than an ordinary "roust". Nitti immediately went into emergency surgery, and by the next morning he still clung to life. Anton Cermak watched and waited for "the grim reaper to finish off the one man who stood between him and his takeover of the Chicago rackets.

Harry Pierpont

Harry Pierpont was a partner of notorious gangster John Dillinger. He was electrocuted at the Columbus, Ohio penitentiary at 12:09 a.m. on Oct. 17, 1934

While Frank Nitti stubbornly held on to the thinnest thread of life, a number of his lesser known lieutenants were making weekly "pilgrimages" to the Indiana State Prison at nearby Michigan City. They visited with Harry Pierpont and Homer Van Meter, a pair of incarcerated bank robbers, and Johnny Dillinger, their eager convict "trainee".

Dillinger had drawn concurrent sentences of two to 14 years, and ten to 20 years for the aborted robbery in 1924 of a Mooresville grocer. Dillinger began his sentence at the Indiana State Reformatory at Pendleton, but was transferred to the State Prison in 1929 when he convinced the Parole Board that his talents as a baseball player might be better nurtured in the "more mature" environment of "the Big House."

Of course, what Dillinger had in mind was working on the details of forming up his legendary bank robbery gang while he finished doing his time. The Chicago "outfit" recognized "talent" when they saw it, and Nitti's "lieutenants" were follow-

Johnny Dillinger

ing through on Frank's plan to have a piece of the action when Harry Pierpont and Homer Van Meter were again on the streets. Meeting up with Johnny Dillinger was an unanticipated "bonus". Of course, Nitti and company were also well aware that a free-lance group of grassroots bank robbers, murderous though they might be, would draw page one press coverage; just what the doctor ordered to take the heat off the "outfit" and shelter its activities, at least for a time, from public scrutiny.

Frank Nitti defied the odds and not only survived, but miraculously recovered to walk out of the hospital within a few months, feeling better than ever. Questions had immediately arisen concerning the gun Nitti had supposedly drawn on Cermak's detectives. Nitti denied having ever seen the gun before, and a Board of Inquiry was convened to consider whether the detectives had been justified in using their weapons on Frank "the Enforcer" Nitti.

The detectives were "whitewashed" and charges of resisting arrest were brought against Nitti. Those charges were lost in trial and post trial procedures, and when the smoke cleared there remained the strong aroma that Nitti had been set up by detectives playing "assassin" for the Mayor. While Nitti convalesced, half the beer distributorships in Chicago became the territory of Roger Touhy, and his mayoral "undisclosed principal".

It seemed as if Anton Cermak had won after all. With Frank Nitti and the Chicago "outfit" apparently neutralized, "his honor," the Mayor, again turned to his "war" against the mainline bankers who had used "Big Bill" Thompson's deposits of City money to shore up their faltering portfolios in Sam Insull's now worthless stock. Cermak's flying squads made the rounds of every bank board room in Cook County, and everywhere their refrain was the same put up, or pay up!

* * *

Increasingly, the lights burned into the wee small hours in the exclusive clubs that were the retreats of the "big rich" in Chicago, as the mainline money men debated what to do about the troublesome Anton Cermak. No one knows quite when "the deal" was struck, but in the early **Autumn of 1932**, an unholy alliance had been formed between the Chicago "outfit" and the beleaguered bankers, fueled by their mutual resolve that Anton Cermak had to go. "Gunner" Jack McGurn, who counted the St. Valentine's Day massacre as notches on his gun, was put in charge of the Cermak disposal problem by Nitti and friends. McGurn decided that Cermak should be put down in a public place, for all to see, so that the message would never be lost on any future politician who decided to become enterprising at the expense of "the outfit".

The Cubs were in the 1932 World Series against the New York Yankees. The Yankees took the first two games in New York and the Cubs came home to Wrigley Field, seeking revenge in Game #3. The '32 Yankees still featured the awesome bat of Babe Ruth, the aging Sultan of Swat; but increasingly the burden of carrying the team was falling to steady Lou Gehrig, a superstar in his own right.

Jack McGurn (above) was hired by the Chicago Outfit to kill Chicago Mayor Anton Cermak.

The word was out that Mayor Cermak would attend the game and sit in a box near home plate. Gunner Jack McGurn knew the field and its surroundings like the back of his hand. A rifleman atop one of the buildings behind the left centerfield wall would have a clean shot at the unsuspecting Mayor as he sat in his box to take in the game.

McGurn's man was in place as the game began. There was a steady stream of well wishers and party faithful who stopped by the Mayor's box during the game. "Too risky", thought the shooter, who decided to wait for things to quiet down for a "safer" shot later in the game.

By the fifth inning the score was tied, four to four on the strength of Ruth's three run homer. Franklin Delano Roosevelt, the Presidential choice of the Democratic Party, joined Anton Cermak in his private box. Secret Service Agents swarmed around the pair. Babe Ruth walked to the plate in the fifth inning. The Cub players yelled every manner of indignity at him, "Potbelly", "Fatso", and worse. Ruth worked the count to two balls and two strikes; 60,000 fans yelled as one for the mighty Babe to strike out.

Ruth yelled at the Cub pitcher, Charlie Root, **"I'm gonna cut the next pitch right down your throat;"** and as he did... the Babe pointed out to Center field in a gesture now rooted in the folklore of Americana. Root's pitch was a change up that curved low and away. Ruth reached for the pitch, and lined it over the center field wall. The stadium went crazy.

Ruth waved at his tormentors, laughed, exulted, "You lucky, lucky bastard," and took his patented "turkey trot" around the bases. Mayor Cermak and Presidential candidate Roosevelt left the park early, and Gunner Jack McGurn's man never did get the opportunity to get off a clean shot at the Mayor.

Anton Cermak delivered the Cook County vote to Franklin Delano Roosevelt in **November 1932**, and Roosevelt buried Herbert Hoover in a Presidential landslide that was more a vote against Hoover's apparent impotency in the face of the hard times of the widening depression, than an affirmation of pro-Roosevelt sentiment.

Anton Cermak, mayor of Chicago, was the target of several unsuccessful assassination attempts.

Gunner Jack McGurn bided his time as Anton Cermak, perhaps reacting to intelligence that tipped him to the mob plot to get him, made himself increasingly scarce in public. Unexpectedly, year end 1932 presented another opportunity to get the Mayor, and again it was a sporting event.

The Chicago Bears had beaten the Green Bay Packers 9-0, in sub-zero conditions in wind swept Wrigley field on Dec. 11 before only 6,000 hardy fans. The weather worsened in the first days of the following week and the National Football League considered cancelling the championship playoff game scheduled for the following Sunday at Wrigley Field between the Bears, and the Portsmouth (Ohio) Spartans.

Then George Halas came up with an inspired suggestion. Why not play the title game indoors at the Chicago Stadium? The Stadium had hosted the Circus the week before, and some six inches of sod remained on the concrete floors. It would take some alterations to the field and the installation of more sod over the remaining base, but preparations could be completed before Sunday. Both the League and the Spartans consented, and on Sunday, **Dec. 18, 1932**, the Bears squared off against the Spartans inside the Chicago Stadium on a specially marked 80 yard field.

More than 15,000 fans packed into the Stadium to see the game, the Mayor of the City of Chicago among them. This time Jack McGurn's "shooter" stationed himself high atop the Stadium in the girders that supported the roof. Anton Cermak was tightly surrounded by bodyguards and the frequent crowd movements to their feet near the Mayor's box during the game, that the Bears would win, 9-0, again denied the rifleman the clear shot he needed to kill the Mayor. The uneasy truce continued in Chicago between the acquisitive Mayor and the "outfit", that at least for the time being seemed to be coming up second best to Anton J. Cermak.

January 1933 was uneventful. Finally, the Chicago Tribune excitedly trumpeted that none other than Chicago's own Anton J. Cermak would accompany President elect Franklin D. Roosevelt to Miami, where the new President would on Feb. 15, 1933, deliver a major speech. Cermak made sure that his travel plans were widely broadcast.

He would ride the Floridan train to Miami and would pack the train with personal bodyguards in the hope that Nitti's men would blunder onto the train in the expectation of making short work of the unsuspecting Mayor. Nitti's boys apparently fell neatly into Cermak's trap. Louie "Little New York" Campagna boarded the train and took a compartment near the Mayor's. Cermak's private police made short work of Campagna, and the Mayor and his entourage breathed sighs of relief as the Floridan headed south; Cermak even discarding the bullet proof vest he had taken to wearing.

What Cermak did not know was that Gunner Jack McGurn had conquered a life long fear of flying to take a primitive charter plane to Miami, arriving many hours before the Floridan. And what neither McGurn nor Cermak knew was that Joseph Zangara, a mentally disturbed unemployed New Jersey mill hand, was himself headed to Miami to personally "see" that the tenure of the newly elected President was brief indeed.

On the morning of **Feb. 15, 1933**, President Roosevelt, and Anton J. Cermak rode side by side through the streets of Miami in the back seat of an open car. The curb side crowds were huge and enthusiastic. At one point they spilled into the street

Joseph Zangara murdered Chicago Mayor Anton Cermak by accident while attempting to kill President Roosevelt saving Machine Gun Jack McGurn from having to do the job himself for the Chicago Mafia.

and swelled forward to the President's car. At that moment, Gunner Jack McGurn, gun in hand, hidden by a paper bag, was seconds away from taking his shot at the Mayor of Chicago when the diminutive Joseph Zangara burst past him, gun in hand, to get at President Roosevelt. Zangara shouldered people out of his path, knocking others down, until he closed to within eight feet of the President's car. Zangara screamed, "There are too many people starving to death," and fired wildly at Roosevelt.

A woman swung her handbag at Zangara, deflecting his pistol upward. One bullet struck Margaret Kruis, a vacationer; another struck Russell Caldwell, simply a curious bystander. But two shots hit Mayor Anton J. Cermak, who was mortally wounded. Gunner Jack McGurn flashed a sardonic grin and melted away into the crowd. A little mad man had done his dirty work for him.

Joseph Zangara was convicted in a whirlwind trial and sentenced to die in the electric chair on **March 21, 1933**. Anton Cermak lingered until **May 6, 1933**. On his death bed he protested that Zangara's hand had been put in motion by the Chicago "outfit" that was taking vengeance for the attempt on Frank Nitti's life.

Cermak wasn't far wrong, but in this world or the next, it was unlikely he'd ever believe what in fact happened to make unnecessary Gunner Jack McGurn's attempt on his life. Joseph Zangara was madly unrepentant when he went to the electric chair on March 21, 1933, screaming, "If I got out I would kill him (Roosevelt) at once," before finally quieting to say,

"Goodbye. Adios to the world," as the executioner threw the switch.

In Chicago, business quickly returned to "normal". With Cermak dead and buried, his flying squads suddenly found themselves with no legal mandate to continue their pursuit of the missing bank deposits, or the payment of gentlemanly graft in lieu thereof. Frank Nitti's boys made short work of Roger Touhy, quickly framing him on the charge of kidnapping Jake "the Barber" Factor, an international con-man and pal of Al Capone, who in fact had "kidnapped" himself and "lammed" it, to escape extradition to England.

Touhy drew a 99 year sentence for a crime he didn't commit, and served more than 20 years before his "frame" was publicly exposed and he was released. When Touhy was finally released in the fifties, he found to his dismay that the memory of the Chicago "outfit" was long indeed, as within a month after his release an unknown gunman shot him, resulting in a leg wound that unfortunately for Touhy severed an artery and killed him.

Nitti once again sat atop Capone's empire, and ran it from the fifth floor of the Wacker-La Salle Building for the next decade. Johnny Dillinger was paroled in **May of 1933**, and with Nitti's underwriting, launched upon his legendary bank robbing spree that appeared to end on **July 22, 1934** when Dillinger, betrayed by Polly Hamilton and Anna Sage, the legendary "lady in red", fell to ambush by East Chicago policemen and FBI agents outside the Biograph Theatre in Chicago. Or did he? In Chicago "appearances" had a strange way of being quite deceiving.

Chapter 6

The Mob and Johnny Dillinger

The Making of a Legend

The Mob and Johnny Dillinger
The Making of a Legend

On the evening of **July 22, 1934**, John Dillinger, Anna Sage, and Polly Hamilton entered the Biograph Theatre in downtown Chicago to see "Manhattan Melodrama", the new Clark Gable film. By 10:30 p.m., the film was approaching its conclusion. William Powell played a "prosecutor" who had convicted his trouble prone "gambler" friend, Clark Gable, of murder. In a final gesture of friendship, Powell offered to spare his pal the death penalty with a recommendation for life imprisonment. Gable, with characteristic bravado, declined the offer, telling his friend that he'd rather die at once than "by inches" for the balance of his life in prison. The final frames showed Gable walking to "the chair".

The film completed, Dillinger and the two women walked out of the "cooled" Biograph, and into the steamy hot

On the evening of July 22, 1934, John Dillinger was cut down in a fusillade of police bullets as he left the Biograph Theatre, pictured at left.

Chicago night. Anna Sage wore red that night to "mark'" her for the FBI agents to whom she had betrayed John Dillinger.

Within seconds Dillinger was cut down in a fusillade of police bullets, and thus ended the greatest manhunt in the United State history.

From the beginning there were loose ends concerning the shooting of Dillinger at the Biograph. As the years passed the debate continued about what really happened in the ambush at the Biograph. The betrayal of Dillinger had been positively devilish, or so it seemed, then. Increasingly it has become apparent that if indeed the "devil" did take a hand in the life and times of John Dillinger, the final chapter was not at all what it seemed on that hot, humid night in Chicago in July of 1934.

John Herbert Dillinger was Indiana born and bred, a product of the depression era midwest. Home was Mooresville, a sleepy farm town, 20 miles southwest of Indianapolis. With his mother Mollie dead in his third year, Dillinger was raised for a time by his red haired older sister Audrey, who, with his father John Wilson Dillinger, would remain his loyal friend and confidant through the turbulent years to come.

The State House in Indiana had only years before been practically captive to the Ku Klux Klan. The twenties brought a new "alienation", this time from the Wall Street financial elite that was bleeding the life from rural America. The malignant cities, and the banks and bankers who funneled farmer dollars east to finance them, were "the enemy" to the failed farmers of the "dust bowl" mid west, and the Indiana "near" mid west.

John Dillinger was born into these times an angry individualist, a "maverick" from the egg. Generally too restless to hold any job for more than a few months, Dillinger's first and abiding love was baseball. His contemporaries agreed that Dillinger had the right stuff to make the big leagues, but time and circumstance dealt him an entirely different hand. The events of the evening of July 21, 1923 were symbolic of the course that Dillinger's life would follow.

John Dillinger occasionally attended the evening service at the Friends Church in Mooresville. This night he waited outside and observed Oliver Macy and his wife arrive and park their new car.

Depressed and angry, needing the freedom of flight on the open road, Dillinger turned his back on the evening service and fired up the Macy car for a two day joy ride through middle Indiana which eventually ended in Indianapolis. Macy and the police caught up with him there, but since Dillinger was a neighborhood boy, Macy declined to press charges.

Shamed and panicky, Dillinger departed Mooresville to join the navy, serving on the battleship Utah. When his inability to cope with the regimen of the Navy, and romantic entanglements that got the better of him, Dillinger simply walked off his ship in Boston and went AWOL, ultimately escaping military justice by returning to Indiana where the navy apparently never thought to look for him.

In September of 1924, Dillinger and another man staged a robbery of their hometown grocer in Mooresville, Indiana. The grocer had been menaced and finally cracked across the forehead with a gun. The rough stuff didn't sit well with Dillinger, and he confided what had happened to his father who persuaded him to come clean with the authorities. Dillinger did so without a lawyer. Leniency was promised, but when judgment was passed Dillinger received the severe sentence of ten to 20 years. His co-defendant who had sought counsel was sentenced to less than half that, and was out within two years.

Dillinger began serving his sentence in the Indiana State Reformatory, but succeeded in winning a transfer to the State Penitentiary in Michigan City by persuading sympathetic prison officials that his talent for playing baseball would be better served at the "state pen" where the inmates participated in organized baseball leagues.

The Indiana State Penitentiary at Michigan City was nestled behind the deserted dunes of Lake Michigan, only 45 miles from the downtown Loop in Chicago. Jail time for Dillinger, then #13225 in the 2,500 man prison population, could have been a day to day straight-jacket, the boredom broken only by baseball games in the yard and the Old Gold broadcasts of Paul Whiteman and his legendary cornetist, Bix Beiderbecke, from WABC in New York; and the championship fight broadcasts of Chicago's own Barney Ross against Tony Canzoneri.

In Michigan City, however, it wasn't only baseball and radio broadcasts that occupied Dillinger's time. From day one Dillinger devoted himself to learning the fine art of robbing banks from accommodating fellow convicts.

Dillinger, a model prisoner, quickly joined the clique of Handsome Harry Pierpont, an Indiana bank robber of some reputation. Pierpont literally taught Dillinger everything he needed to know to become a legendary bank robber. Pierpont's gang behind the walls included Homer Van Meter, John Hamilton, and Charles Makley.

Almost from the beginning of his jail term, there was strong sentiment that Dillinger had received an unduly severe sentence. Eventually, even his sentencing Judge, J. W. Williams, joined in a petition by some 200 citizens of his hometown, Mooresville, Indiana, for a commutation of his sentence. Governor Paul V. McNutt signed Executive Order No. 7723, on **May 10, 1933**, setting Dillinger's release date for the last week in May.

With his parole imminent in the Spring of 1933, Pierpont armed Dillinger with a list of target banks that would be ripe for plucking. Dillinger was released from the Indiana State Penitentiary at Michigan City on **May 22, 1933**, several days early, when it was learned that his stepmother, Elizabeth Fields, was mortally ill.

Upon his return to Mooresville, Dillinger was warmly greeted by friends and family. Although he was anxious to begin working down Handsome Harry Pierpont's list of banks ripe for picking, Dillinger, ever the affable con man, attended his stepmother's funeral, and the Father's Day services a few weeks later at the local Friend's Church, and assured any of his hometown acquaintances who would listen that he was sick of life on the wrong side of the law, and was going straight. His promises of reform scarcely had cleared his lips when Dillinger began working Handsome Harry's list, robbing banks throughout the mid west to raise enough money to bust his pals out of the Indiana Penitentiary.

Louis Piquett was the lawyer of choice for John Dillinger.

As Dillinger made headlines with his daring bank robberies, law enforcement agencies began pooling their resources for the purpose of putting an end to his crime wave. The press wrote Dillinger up as a depression era robin hood. Dillinger was loving every minute of it.

Matt Leach, the captain of the Indiana State Police, headed up one "get Dillinger" unit. Captain John Stege, of the City of Chicago detective squad, headed up another such unit. Undaunted by the police dragnets, Dillinger taunted his pursuers with telephone calls, at one point calling Leach "a stuttering bastard", and mailing him a book on "How To Be A Detective."

Strangely, though, despite the fact that he was riding high, seemingly always one step ahead of his pursuers, Dillinger, the hay seed bank robber, knew that one day he'd need an "out" from his crime spree, lest he end up another number on a morgue slab. In early summer 1933, John Dillinger made his peace with the Chicago mafia "outfit", meeting with Frank Nitti, and forming a secret partnership that would last a lifetime.

In addition to the tools of his trade, brazen nerve and daring, and a veritable armory of sub-machine guns and hand guns, John Dillinger's first scrape with the law, one that cost him nearly nine years of his life behind bars, taught him never again to be without a lawyer, and a skilled one at that. Louis Piquett was the lawyer of Dillinger's choice.

Piquett was colorful in both appearance and accomplishments. Short of stature with a stocky build, Louis Piquett sported a three inch high salt and pepper pompadour. Piquett never attended law school, but rather began his "legal" training working as a bartender and waiter before graduating to a position as "hanger on" at the police precinct houses, and, eventually "message carrier" between lawyers, their clients, and bail bondsmen.

Finally, Piquett became a "counselor" to ward healers, politicians and underworld characters, and, in the process, "read" enough law to earn his license. In 1933, Louis Piquett not only represented John Dillinger, but also Al Capone, Frank Nitti, and the entire Chicago mob

Frank 'Jelly' Nash was a bank robber and an outfit soldier who was taken into federal custody on June 15, 1933 becoming a liability to the Outfit.

"outfit". When a pal warned Piquett that he'd come to a bad end representing gangsters, Piquett grinned impishly and said he had no choice, stating, "They're the only ones who have money these days."

Al Capone had already begun serving his 11 year jail sentence for tax evasion. Frank Nitti sat alone atop the Chicago underworld. But Frank Nitti had an immediate problem - what to do about Frank "Jelly" Nash, an outfit soldier in federal custody who just might be on the verge of singing.

"Jelly" Nash was a balding bank robber who walked with a limp, and looked anything but the desperado. On July 26 of the prior year, Nash, Fred Barker, and Alvin Karpis electrified the country when they looted the Cloud County Bank at Concordia, Kansas of $240,000 in bonds and cash. The bonds were "washed" by the Chicago "outfit", and "Jelly". Nash went into hiding in one of the underworld's favorite safe places, Hot Springs, Arkansas.

On **June 15, 1933**, "Jelly" Nash was spotted by FBI agents and taken into custody without a shot being fired. Nash had escaped from the Leavenworth federal penitentiary years before and was once again ticketed for the Kansas prison, this time for life.

"Jelly" Nash knew all the connections between the free-lance bank robbers and the Chicago "outfit". Faced with a life sentence, Frank "Jelly" Nash suddenly became a serious liability for the Chicago "outfit", and one that had to be dealt with quickly.

It was Louis Piquett who came up with the novel expedient of putting the mob boss together with the bank robber. Piquett knew that Dillinger was only recently departed from the federal penitentiary system, and still counted close and loyal friends among the inmates. There was something of an "underground telegraph" between cons and their pals on the outside.

Dillinger just might be able to use his contacts to locate "Jelly" Nash for the outfit. Piquett volunteered to act as "intermediary" between Dillinger and Nitti, but Frank Nitti preferred to look into a man's eyes up close and personal when making a deal that might involve life or death. Their meeting was set for a Sunday in June on the grounds of the Chicago World's Fair.

The Chicago World's Fair, the Century of Progress Exhibition, was a sprawl of art deco spires for 86 acres along Lake Michigan, an opulent anomaly sitting defiantly in the path of the westward bound depression. The Sky Ride with its "rocket cars" skimmed above the flat surfaces and modernistic pavilions in pastels between the Eiffel-like towers that marked the Exhibit. The Sinclair Oil plaster dinosaur "menaced" the long lines of visitors that wound their way into the Seminole Indian Village.

Wherever one turned, the sights were garish and spectacular, from the facades of Fortune and Time magazines, two stories high, to a thermometer over 20 stories high. Frank Nitti sat in his limousine at the curb before the General Exhibits Building. John Dillinger walked in the crowd, his girl Mary Longnaker on his arm. Dillinger spotted Nitti's limo, but delayed long enough to ask a policeman to snap a picture of him and Mary. Nitti stepped from his limo thinking that Dillinger might have too much nerve. Dillinger's grin disarmed him, and they walked into the General Exhibits Building.

The foyer was roped off and armed guards ringed a pedestal in the center of the floor that was the focal point of visitor attention. Nitti took his place in line, Dillinger at his side. In minutes they stood before the clear glass dome under which sparkled a million dollars worth of cut diamonds, gem stones ready for setting. Nitti whispered, "More here than in a hundred of your hick banks." Dillinger eyed the guards, and breathed, "Too many guns." Nitti gestured for Dillinger to follow, and outside the General Exhibits Building they entered the limousine. Nitti instructed his driver, "Take us to the Streets of Paris."

They parked outside the red, white, and blue steamship facade and walked through to the narrow "Left Bank" look-alike streets that were lined with sidewalk cafes, complete with striped awnings and little round tables covered by colorful umbrellas. Gendarmes nodded genially. Nitti and Dillinger pushed their way through knots of sightseers, strolling troubadours, chestnut vendors, and flower girls.

A bevy of bathing beauties splashed around the great Lido outdoor pool. Inside the Cafe de la Paix, the maitre de seated them ringside at the polished dance floor. An orchestra played gaily from its seat on the tiered stage behind the dance floor. A chorus line of blonde showgirls, covered by gauzy coverlets, turned pirouettes around the dance floor where Sally Rand would do her famous "fan dance" within the hour.

The men eyed each other, sipping their drinks, and Nitti wasted no time getting to his "proposition". The "outfit" needed to know when Frank "Jelly" Nash was being transported by federal officers. The "word" had it that Nash was in Kansas City. Nitti wanted to free "Jelly" Nash, one way or the other. Dillinger assured Nitti that locating Nash should be no problem. If his pals inside the walls came up short, Pretty Boy Floyd, with whom he'd worked, was in Kansas City and could "finger" Nash.

Dillinger's tone and air of assurance left no doubt in Nitti's mind that he could "deliver". With Nash out of the way, Nitti turned to another subject. The Chicago "outfit" needed to replenish its cache of weapons and bullet proof vests that were used to arm and protect the men who guarded the liquor convoys and also the "soldiers" who did the mob's dirty work.

The Dillinger gang had been known on occasion to raid armories. Dillinger agreed to provide the "outfit" whatever guns it needed. In return, Nitti would open to Dillinger the outfit's money laundering services of Boss McLaughlin and Jimmy Probasco, to wash the dirty money, bonds, and securities Dillinger "withdrew" from his banks.

Dillinger then got to his real reason for meeting with Nitti. Dillinger knew that in time he would need a new identity to elude the ever tightening police dragnet dogging his trail. The "outfit" was known to specialize in such services, including plastic surgery and fingerprint removal. As Dillinger spoke, Nitti had a brainstorm and said, "What you want is no problem, but, Johnny boy, we should be able to do you even one better." Nitti described what he had in mind, and Dillinger grinned broadly.

June 17, 1933, Union Station, Kansas City. John Dillinger "learned" that Nash would be returned to Leavenworth on June 17, 1933, and, as agreed, passed that information on to the Chicago "outfit". Frank Nitti immediately dispatched *Verne* Miller and Adam Richetti to see Nash off on his trip from Kansas City to Leavenworth.

Nash, the Police Chief of McAlester, Oklahoma, two Kansas City policemen, and four FBI agents were in a car at the curb at the Union Station in Kansas City when Nitti's gunmen caught up with them. Miller and Richetti approached the car and under the pretext of attempting to "free" Nash, opened fire on the agents and policemen. Frank "Jelly" Nash was "accidently" killed in the first volley, as was one FBI special agent, the McAlester police chief, and the two Kansas City policemen. Two other FBI special agents were also wounded.

Newspapers carried the story of the "Kansas City Massacre" as a spectacular attempted break out that failed. In Washington, D.C., J. Edgar Hoover, the director of the FBI, was incensed. Hoover saw the mob's hand behind the massacre and instructed his field office in Chicago to get on the case and break it open.

When Dillinger "fingered" Nash, Frank Nitti considered his deal with the bank robber sealed, and turned to his side of the "bargain". Nitti maintained a suite of rooms at the Bismarck Hotel in the Loop at the corner of La Salle and Randolph, across the street from City Hall. It was there that Nitti summoned his lawyer, Louis Piquett, and Willie Bioff for a meeting.

Willie Bioff was a member of Al Capone's gang and worked for the Hollywood stagehands' union, the IATSE (International Alliance for Theatrical Stage Employees). Bioff, a stocky Russian-American, was the head of the southern California branch. In the 1930's, Bioff's name became synonymous with Hollywood labor corruption.

Willie Bioff was a fat little man who wore wire framed glasses, and attempted to dress "nattily" with loud ties and black silk suits. A former union "slugger", Bioff had graduated to "overseer" of the extensive prostitution cribs run by the "outfit" in Chicago. Although he craved "respect" from his criminal "peers", Bioff could never shake the "pimp" tag and a reputation for slapping his girls around.

Nitti spelled out his deal with Dillinger, and informed his lieutenants that Dillinger indeed did deliver Nash, as promised. Bioff was somewhat surprised at Frank Nitti's "about face" on the subject of farmer bank robbers. Nitti had often said that the bank robbers were "bad for business" in that they tended to bring the "heat" of law enforcement down on all criminal activities. On this day, however, Frank Nitti turned his argument 180 degrees, saying that when the Dillingers grabbed the headlines they kept the "outfit" off the front page, and that wasn't all bad.

Nitti then asked Willie Bioff about one of his boys, a man named Jimmy Lawrence. Bioff answered that Lawrence was a "nobody" with a bum heart who worked at the Bucket of Blood speakeasy in the Kostur Hotel in East Chicago, Indiana. Louis Piquett volunteered, "That's Anna Sage's place," and Nitti nodded, "Yeah, I know." Willie Bioff was then dismissed.

Louis Piquett waited on Nitti for an explanation concerning his sudden interest in one, Jimmy Lawrence. Nitti explained simply, "Lawrence looks a little like Dillinger," then directed Piquett to "see to it that Jimmy Lawrence looks exactly like Dillinger." Piquett knew better than to press for details. Jimmy Probasco, one of the "outfits" money launderers, had been a veterinarian, and doubled as a plastic surgeon for the mob.

Piquett left his meeting with Nitti, and passed the word to both Probasco and Lawrence as to what Nitti had in mind. Jimmy Lawrence was uneasy, but knew better than to question Frank Nitti. But Nitti, ever the diplomat, learning that Jimmy Lawrence had let slip his "concerns", summoned Lawrence to a meeting at the Villa Capri, and explained that if one Dillinger was in the headlines robbing banks, why not "create" another to rob other banks for the "outfit", leaving the real John Dillinger to take the rap for all the stick ups.

Besides, it was well known that Lawrence had fallen hard for one of Anna Sage's "ladies", Polly Hamilton, and was concerned that Polly be taken care of when his rheumatic "bad heart" finally gave out. If their plan misfired, Frank Nitti assured Jimmy Lawrence that Polly Hamilton would never want for anything. Nitti chuckled, "Everybody, dies, right Jimmy?" Lawrence got "the message", and decided to go along with the program. His doubts thus taken care of, Lawrence left Nitti eager to submit to "the surgeons" knife.

John Dillinger continued to do what he did best - rob banks - and also to find a way to break "Handsome Harry" Pierpont and "friends" out of jail. Dillinger's first attempt to spring his pals proved unsuccessful when guns he'd thrown over the prison walls were discovered by other inmates and turned in to the warden. Undaunted, Dillinger next, in late September, 1933, hid guns in a barrel of thread that was "ticketed" for the Michigan City Penitentiary shirt factory. The barrel was marked with a red "x", and Dillinger waited on its delivery.

But on **Sept. 22, 1933**, police received a tip that Dillinger would be visiting his girlfriend, Mary Longnaker, in Dayton, Ohio. Longnaker's apartment was staked out, and John Dillinger was apprehended when he showed up.

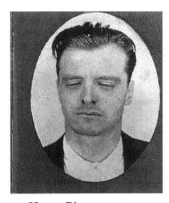

Harry Pierpont murdered Sheriff Jess Sarber

In a strange "turn-about" Dillinger was behind bars in the Lima, Ohio, jail on **Sept. 26, 1933** when "Handsome Harry" Pierpont and his gang finally "took delivery" of their guns and successfully crashed out of the Indiana State Penitentiary.

Finally on the "outside", "Handsome Harry" Pierpont's first order of business was springing his pal John Dillinger from the Lima, Ohio, jail. Dillinger was already a bona fide folk hero, and the Lima Sheriff, Jess Sarber, struck up a friendship with the personable bank robber and gave him the run of the jail building, under guard.

It was the evening of **Oct. 12, 1933**, Columbus Day, minutes after Sheriff Sarber's wife Lucy had served Dillinger his supper, when Harry Pierpont and friends burst through the jail door and demanded to see the prisoner on the pretext that they were policemen that came to extradite him to Chicago. Sheriff Jess Sarber demanded to see his visitors "ID" and credentials. Harry Pierpont impatiently repeated his demand to see Dillinger, and when Jess Sarber continued to delay, Pierpont pulled his pistol and fatally shot Sarber in the belly.

Other gang members released Dillinger from his cell, but Dillinger refused to leave when he saw Mrs. Sarber cradling her dying husband. Harry Pierpont pulled at Dillinger's arm, yelling at him to get moving to the getaway car outside. As Sheriff Jess Sarber breathed his last, Dillinger finally followed Pierpont to the car, snapping angrily, "Did you have to do that?"

Harry Pierpont could have challenged Dillinger for leadership of their reconstituted gang, but he always deferred to the flamboyant bank robber. For his part, Dillinger seemed to relish being in the limelight. Dillinger saw himself as a country boy bank robber, making war on the banks and bankers who in his eyes created the depression. Harry Pierpont was as close a friend as Dillinger would ever have, but on several occasions Dillinger came close to calling out Pierpont on the issue of gratuitous violence. Killing might be unavoidable when the other side had drawn guns or started the shooting, but Dillinger hated drawing blood unnecessarily. Besides, in his view, it was bad for business, and dangerous at that.

As Dillinger explained to his father, "Something you don't have to worry about, Dad. I never killed a man and never will. You shoot at a man and cripple him and he might kill you. But if you shoot close and just scare him, he's gone." After Jess Sarber, Dillinger made it clear that the next man who fired a shot when not in legitimate fear of getting shot, would answer to him personally.

In hiding again, the gang considered its options. Harry Pierpont had cased the Central National Bank at Greencastle, Indiana, and advised his pals it should be "easy pickings". Dillinger agreed, but first the gang pulled a raid on the police arsenal at Peru, Indiana, on **Oct. 20, 1933**, to fill a weapons 'order' from the Chicago 'outfit'. Dillinger personally delivered the weapons, including handguns, Winchester rifles, machine guns, and sawed off shotguns, to Chicago, before rejoining his gang in Greencastle.

The Greencastle bank job went off without a hitch on **October 23, 1933**. Dillinger, as was his custom, dressed "to the nines" in a natty suit and "straw boater", and "performed" his patented leap over the teller railing to personally "rifle" the cash drawers. The bank raid, for all intents and purposes, finished, Dillinger strolled past an old farmer who was standing at one of the teller's cages, a stack of bills before him. The money caught Dillinger's eye and he asked the farmer, "That your money or the bank's?"

The farmer replied, "Mine," and Dillinger walked on by, grinning, "Keep it. We only want the bank's." The "take" at Greencastle was more than $75,000 in cash and bonds. In the aftermath of the Greencastle job, Matt Leach, the head of the Indiana State Police detachment tracking Dillinger, held a press conference in which he assured reporters that Dillinger's days were numbered.

When Leach returned to his office, his phone rang and he was shocked to hear Dillinger himself on the line. Leach was speechless. Dillinger seized the moment arrogantly shouting,

"This is John Dillinger. How are you, you stuttering bastard?"

It was in this period that Dillinger contracted a skin rash known as "barber's itch". Dillinger had business in the Chicago vicinity, and while there, planned to visit Dr. Charles Eye for treatment. The Chicago police received a tip that Dillinger would be showing up at Dr. Eye's, and on the night of **Nov. 15, 1933** they lay in wait for Dillinger at Dr. Eye's office on Irving Park Boulevard.

Dillinger first picked up new girlfriend, Billie Frechette, and with Billie at his side, John Dillinger drove his Hudson Essex Teraplane to Park Boulevard. Dillinger immediately sensed that there was something wrong. There were too many cars on the street, and two were facing the wrong way. Smelling the ambush, Dillinger dropped the Hudson into "reverse" and roared back the way he'd come. A wild chase ensued, with police firing shotguns as they pulled close to the Hudson Teraplane, but no one handled the wheel better than Johnny Dillinger when the lead was flying.

At one point his pursuers surely thought they had him, as two trolley cars heading toward each other on parallel tracks converged to cut off Dillinger's escape. But Dillinger roared through the rapidly narrowing space between the cars, and in short order, outdistanced his pursuers, finally losing them by "nosing" the Hudson into a narrow alley. It had been a close call, but Dillinger still had important business in the Chicago vicinity.

Satisfied that he had lost the police, Dillinger drove into East Chicago, Indiana and parked in an alley near the Kostur Hotel. Dillinger dipped into a make-up kit that rested on the seat between him and Billie Frechette, and stuck on a large mustachio and curly haired wig. Billy grinned, "My Mex", and Dillinger instructed her to be ready to start the car if he came running. As Dillinger walked down the alley, heading for the basement entrance to the Kostur Hotel, he picked up sounds of screams, women's screams, coming from an adjoining building.

A shadowy figure emerged from a dimly lit doorway, and Dillinger found himself eye to eye with Willie Bioff. The usually dapper pimp was in a sweat, his clothes disheveled.

Bioff pushed on by Dillinger, muttering, "Mind your own business, soldier, before you get a taste of what them whores got." As Bioff exited the alley, Dillinger retraced his steps to the basement entrance of the Kostur Hotel, and there entered the "Bucket of Blood" speakeasy.

Louie "Little New York" Campagna, Frank Nitti's body-guard, covered the door, eyed Dillinger intently, before nodding silently in recognition and finally admitting him. Dillinger blinked at the smokey light in the basement bar, and then moved across the room to drop into a chair at a table beside one occupied by Frank Nitti. Their backs "faced" each other, but they could speak and be heard without appearing to be in con-versation.

Nitti directed Dillinger's attention to the bar, saying, "What do you think, kid?" Dillinger eyed the bartender as Nitti explained, "That's Jimmy Lawrence." Dillinger grinned, shak-ing his head. There was a resemblance. Nitti's plan might work. Maybe. Dillinger reached under his jacket, and picking himself up to leave, dropped a money belt onto his chair. Nitti motioned to Louie Campagna, who retrieved the money belt as Dillinger made his way out of the speakeasy.

John Dillinger caught up with his gang in Milwaukee, Wisconsin, where "Handsome Harry" Pierpont had scouted out a job in Racine. It was near closing time on **Nov. 20, 1933** at the American Bank and Trust Company in Racine, when Harry Pierpont walked in and pasted up a huge red cross poster over the largest picture window in the bank. Once the "red cross" flashed out the window, and kept out inquiring eyes, Dillinger and the rest of the gang hurried in to make their unscheduled "withdrawal." Head Teller Harold Graham didn't move quickly enough in delivering the bank's money to the gang, and his "tardiness" earned him a bullet in the elbow from an impatient bank robber.

As Graham fell, he wildly reached out for the counter and set off a silent alarm that sounded at the Racine Police Headquarters. Two policemen responded, but with no real ur-gency since they were convinced that "as usual" it had been the ancient wiring at the bank "sounding" the false alarm. The policemen nonchalantly walked into the bank and to their surprise found themselves facing the drawn weapons of the Dillinger gang.

In the ensuing scuffle, one of the policemen, Wilbur Hansen, was shot, the other disarmed by Dillinger who jammed his pistol under the man's ribs, and ushered him in, saying, "Come on in and join us." Twenty-seven thousand, seven hundred and eighty-nine dollars richer, John Dillinger, Harry Pierpont, and their gang exited American Bank and Trust, holding Mrs. Henry Patzke, the bookkeeper, and the bank's president, hostage.

When the gang was clear of town, Dillinger directed his driver to pull over. He grinned at Mrs. Patzke, and said, "Maybe we ought to take you along. Can you cook?" Mrs. Patzke replied "After a fashion," and Dillinger smiled as he ushered her and the bank president out of the car, saying, "Some other time."

As they pulled away, a tune played on the radio, and the gang of men burst into howls of laughter at the lyric, "John Dillinger was the man for me, He robbed the Glendale train, Took from the banks, gave to the poor, Shan't see his like again."

Chapter 7
Crown Point

Then Little Bohemia

Crown Point, Then Little Bohemia

Dillinger then decided that his gang should drop out of sight for a time, and to a man, they packed their bags, to head south to Daytona Beach for the winter. On **Dec. 20, 1933**, before leaving, Dillinger couldn't resist taunting his pursuers. He called Matt Leach and asked him how his search for the Dillinger gang was progressing.

Then Dillinger telephoned Sergeant Reynolds, the head field operative of Captain John Stege's "Dillinger" squad of City of Chicago policemen, and told him, "You'd better watch your ass." The garrulous Reynolds replied, "We'll take you", and offered to meet Dillinger alone any time, any where. Dillinger laughed at Reynolds, and clicked off.

In Florida, Dillinger arranged for seaside cottages, and the bank robbers settled in for water, sun, and quiet days and nights out of harm's way, listening to the radio. Dillinger's motives in heading south were not entirely therapeutic. Within a few days he headed across country to El Paso. Reaching El Paso, he drove a few miles farther west to Sutter's Well, an old silver mining center that had been a ghost town for years.

Dillinger walked the dusty main street as the gusting wind blew creosote bushes and mesquite balls around him. The man he had traveled so far to meet was a half hour late, but finally he appeared and handed over the passport and papers. More importantly, he then guided Dillinger to the southerly edge of the ghost town.

He smiled, "This is good country for outlaws." Dillinger raised his eyebrows, and the man explained, "This was Pancho Villa territory." Dillinger drawled, "He's been dead more than a few years, hasn't he amigo?" "Some men never die, senor," said the Mexican. "When Villa was killed in 1923, his men could not endure the end of the exciting times on the trail with him."

"That so," smiled Dillinger. "He rise from the dead?" "Those closest to Villa exhumed his body," the Mexican explained, "and took his head. They put it in a huge glass jar of rum and hid it under a pile of orange rocks in the Van Horn mountains." The Mexican pointed back in their direction. "Then what," asked Dillinger.

"On many nights they would take out Villa's head, and smoke peyote and marijuana, and drink mescal with him." "Villa lives, eh," said the American bank robber. The Mexican shrugged his shoulders, and gestured south, beyond Juarez, deep into Chihuahua, saying, "That's the border crossing trail into Mexico. There's no police, no customs, no crossing post. You just walk across. It's as simple as that." Dillinger paid him the $5,000, as agreed, and chuckled as he left Sutter's Well that Frank Nitti indeed had the connections he said he did — even in the middle of nowhere, and near a rock pile that covered Pancho Villa's head!

Thinking about the bandit leader, Dillinger called back to the Mexican, "Not exactly my idea of living forever, pardner?" The Mexican waved, "Who's to say", and shuffled off into the blowing dust and mesquite. Dillinger crossed over into Mexico, and spent most of the next 30 days scouting the area for future reference.

After **New Years 1934**, John Dillinger drove to Tucson, Arizona, where he hooked up with Harry Pierpont and other gang members who had come west from Florida to spend the remainder of the winter in the southwest. The sojourn in Tucson proved to be a blunder for John Dillinger and Harry Pierpont, for the latter, an episode that eventually proved fatal.

In Tucson, the gang dispersed in twos and threes to different boarding houses. As luck would have it, one of the boarding houses burned down, and as the fire raged, two nervous bank robbers, Charles Makley and Russell Clark, paid Tucson fireman William Benedict several hundred dollars to re-enter the inferno, and rescue their suitcase from Room 329.

Benedict succeeded in re-entering the room and found the suitcase. He ran to the window and was about to drop it out the window when Makley and Clark spotted him and screamed, "Don't throw it!" Benedict walked the suitcase out, but as suspicions aroused, he and other firemen then checked the contents of the unnaturally heavy suitcase and discovered submachine guns and other firearms.

The two members of the Dillinger gang were quickly arrested. Headlines boldly proclaimed that the Dillinger gang had been broken. The newsprint was premature, by days, but in the end, not far from wrong. Other townspeople, their suspicions aroused after comparing the appearance of a group of strangers to a photo spread on the Dillinger gang in the True Detective magazine, alerted police, and by **Jan. 23, 1934**, the entire gang, John Dillinger included, was behind bars.

Before being returned to Chicago by plane, Dillinger was interviewed by Tubby Toms of the Indianapolis News. Fingering a rabbit's foot, Dillinger grinned, "My luck's beginning to run out," then kidded, "I shot him out of season. I guess I'm just a born criminal."

In Chicago, Dillinger was bundled into a car with his nemesis, Sergeant Reynolds, and driven in a 13 car police caravan, escorted by a dozen motorcycle troopers, to Indiana. Thousands of curious Dillinger watchers lined the streets as the bank robber's motorcade rolled through each small township along the way.

.   In short order, the entire Dillinger gang was returned to Indiana with the exception of Handsome Harry Pierpont, who was extradited to Ohio where he was charged with the murder of Sheriff Jess Sarber in the earlier bust out of Dillinger from the Lima, Ohio jail. Dillinger was finally incarcerated in the impregnable three story brick Lake County Jail at Crown Point, Indiana, where he was to stand trial for the murder of officer Patrick O'Malley during the Jan. 15, 1934 robbery of the First National Bank of East Chicago, Indiana.

From the first, Dillinger protested that he had been in the southwest since New Years, and could not have committed the East Chicago robbery. At Crown Point, Dillinger received a visit from his attorney, Louis Piquett, who confirmed what Dillinger already had surmised. The $20,736 robbery of the First National Bank of East Chicago, Indiana was pulled by a Dillinger look-a-like gang, led by none other than Jimmy Lawrence. Martin Zarkovich and Tim O'Neill, respectively, Sergeant and Captain of East Chicago detectives, and trusted henchmen of Frank Nitti, were also in on the robbery.

Louis Piquett

Piquett smiled knowingly, saying, "The East Chicago cops pulled that one with Lawrence figuring one more on your tab wouldn't make any difference." But it wasn't the robbery that troubled Dillinger. "I don't want to swing for a murder I didn't commit." His lawyer grinned knowingly, and assured him, "You won't, Johnny boy, you won't."

Time clearly was needed to put in motion an escape plan, and Piquett succeeded in persuading Judge Murray to grant a trial continuance to **March 12, 1934**. As he walked from the courtroom, Piquett quipped to the prosecutor that he needed the extra time in any event to fence $40,000 in hot bonds from the Greencastle robbery that Dillinger had turned over to him for his fee.

Dillinger's captivity created a circus atmosphere at Crown Point. The jail was believed to be escape proof, and gangs of heavily armed Farmers' Protective Association vigilantes roamed the grounds as back up for the dozens of National Guardsmen, local policemen, and state policemen guarding the jail. On more than one occasion, Dillinger posed for the cameras of ever present news reporters, one picture showing him grinning sardonically at the camera in the company of Sheriff Lillian Holley, and the District Attorney.

Dillinger received visits from his family, and also from Sergeant Martin Zarkovich of the East Chicago, Indiana Police Department. Zarkovich' presence was explained as interest in the shooting of Patrick O'Malley during the robbery of the First National Bank of East Chicago, Indiana, a shooting which Dillinger steadfastly denied.

In fact, Zarkovich had been sent to visit Dillinger by the Chicago "outfit" and to slip him a handgun. It was Dillinger who hit upon the expedient of covering his possession of a real weapon, and shielding Zarkovich from later questions, by carving a phony gun from the top of a washboard and darkening it with bootblack.

On the night of **March 2, 1934**, a small plane made three low altitude passes over the jail at Crown Point, each time gunning its *engine as* it roared over the jail. It was a harbinger of things to come. Less than 24 hours later, on the morning of **March 3, 1934**, Dillinger flashed the "gun", and succeeded in disarming a deputy and jail attendant.

Armed with weapons taken from the guards, the Zarkovich pistol now hidden under his shirt, Dillinger was able to make good his escape, convincing reporters that he had pulled it off with the phony gun. Dillinger rounded up more than a dozen guards, jamming them into his cell, and then released Herbert Youngblood, a black men being held for murder. Holding two hostages, Dillinger drove Sheriff Holley's car across the back roads of Indiana and into Illinois.

Once across the state line, Dillinger released his hostages and gave them $4.00 for carfare and food, apologizing, "I'd give you guys more, but that's all I can spare." As he drove away, the hostages swore that they heard the bank robber singing, "I'm heading for the last round-up." The interstate theft of Sheriff Holley's car officially brought the FBI into the chase, although FBI agents had been working with local police for months in tracking Dillinger.

Dillinger's first order of business was putting together another gang to rob banks. In order to do that, Dillinger headed to St. Paul, Minnesota where he was joined by his girlfriend, Billie Frechette, and the nucleus of his new gang, Homer Van Meter and John Hamilton, the only member of the prior gang who had managed to escape the police cordon in Tucson.

All that was missing was a gunner, a trigger happy character, whose menace both ordinary-citizens and bank guards would learn to fear.

It was the Chicago "outfit" that provided the gunman the gang needed for the inevitable rough stuff in the person of one Lester Gillis, a California bootlegger with an uncanny facility with automatic weapons. Gillis had earned his spurs guarding liquor convoys for the mob, and soon he was known exclusively by his criminal stage name, Baby Face Nelson.

Lester Gillis (a,k,a, Baby Face Nelson)

The gang's next target was the Security National Bank and Trust Company in Sioux Falls, South Dakota. On **March 5, 1934**, John Hamilton entered the town alone, introducing himself as a movie producer who would be using locals and their police as extras the following day in shooting a gangster film. Joined by the remainder of his "film crew" the next day, **March 6, 1934**, Hamilton, Dillinger and company lined up the police and townspeople outside the bank as willing extras in what they believed was the filming of a bank robbery. Dillinger then entered the bank and proceeded to make a $49,000 withdrawal.

While his gang cased the First National Bank in Mason City, Iowa, Johnny Dillinger left them to keep an appointment in Chicago. Dillinger drove his Hudson Teraplane through Chicago's west side, and rolled to a stop on Malden, a four block street connecting the Graceland Cemetery and the St. Boniface Cemetery. The street was tree lined, and the still barren limbs swayed in the sharp breezes blowing in off Lake Michigan. Dillinger stepped out of the Hudson, lit up a cigar, and lounged on the fender, waiting.

In minutes, a Cadillac limousine pulled onto Malden, and parked a block up the street from the Hudson. Frank Nitti left the limo and walked down the street toward Dillinger, who moved to meet him half way. The two men shook hands, and Nitti said, "There's a lot of heat from Stege and that Indiana cop, Leach. Hoover's G-Men are all over the place too. I guess he's looking to grab some ink when you cash in. Dillinger chuckled, "And when will that be, Frank?"

Nitti flashed a sardonic grin, "Soon, my son, soon." "Anything I can do for you, Frank," asked Dillinger. "If you happen to pass an armory on the way to your next bank, why don't you stop in and make a purchase - for your friends." "Sure thing, Frank, sure thing," said Dillinger, who added, "There should be some pretty good chunks of dough, too." "That's good," said Nitti. "It's the dough that buys you what you want in this world."

Nitti gestured up the street. "That's St. Boniface Cemetery. A lot of good people rest there. Your kind of people, my kind of people." Nitti turned, and pointed in the other direction. "Now down there is Graceland, my son. That's where the bluebloods get planted. A few years ago, they had to bury old railroad George Pullman in a lead lined coffin under a 20 ton blanket of concrete and steel because he was so popular with all the workers he'd screwed. Even at that, some of the union guys were going to blow the bastard out of the ground. The tight asses had to call on us to talk to the union and call them off."

Nitti, smiling broadly, stated, "They wanted to pay, but shit, I had them dead nuts, you know what I mean. Hell, I said, it's on the house, and now they owe me one. And you know what, my son, the big shots don't like that." Nitti took his leave, and Dillinger remained in Chicago for the balance of the day, later picking up a police tail that mushroomed into a high speed chase before he was able to give his pursuers the slip in the East Chicago switching yards.

Dillinger was with his gang on **March 13, 1934**, in Mason City, Iowa, when they took down the First National Bank. Decades later, Mason City would be immortalized by one of its native sons as the setting for the 'Music Man' musical. First National was rumored to hold $240,000 in cash, and Homer Van Meter literally charged through the front door, brandishing his sub machine gun as he came, so anxious was he to relieve the citizens of Mason City of their money.

The bank president, Willis Bagley, who personally carried the vault key, saw Van Meter charging at him and escaped into his office, locking the door behind him. Van Meter raked the door with sub machine gun bursts, attempting to blow off the lock; but miraculously the lock held, protecting Bagley and depriving the gang of the vault key.

Undaunted, the remainder of the gang entered and began cleaning out the tellers' cages. Bank robberies never seemed to go a little bit wrong. Either they went off without a hitch or they went from bad to worse. Mason City was no exception. A guard, in a special 7-foot steel cage suspended above the lobby, fired a tear gas shell at the floor below, hitting gang member Eddie Green. Green returned the fire, wounding guard Tom Walters in the cage.

A female customer ran from the bank down an adjoining alley, and literally into a small man wearing a cap. She screamed at him, "Get to work and notify somebody, the bank is being held up!" Baby Face Nelson brandished his machine gun and said, "Lady, you're telling me," and pushed her back up the alley and into the bank.

Inside, the gang's attention was directed to the teller's cage before the vault, where cashier Harry Fisher, himself locked in the cage, passed stacks of bills to gang members outside the cage who impatiently threatened to shoot him if he didn't hurry up. What the gang didn't know was that Fisher, running a steel nerved bluff, could have opened the cage and given them immediate access to the vault, even without the key that bank president Bagley had taken with him into the sanctuary of his office.

Outside, Dillinger and Homer Van Meter guarded the street. John Shipley, an elderly policeman, drew a bead on Dillinger from the window of his third floor office above the bank. Winged in the arm, Dillinger immediately returned the favor, spraying the third floor facia of the building with a burst from his sub machine gun. Shipley ducked back in, unhurt. The gang was taking too much time, and Dillinger and Van Meter entered the bank and ordered the remainder of the gang to pull out.

Cashier Fisher breathed a sigh of relief. He had passed the gang $53,344., a substantial amount, but his bluff had deprived them of more than $200,000 still resting safely in the vault. Dillinger and his men piled into a large Buick sedan, and then forced 20 hostages to ride the fenders, running boards, and back bumper of the Buick. Police closed in and began exchanging fire with the gang. Jack Hamilton was hit in the shoulder as he entered the Buick. Baby Face Nelson angrily exploded into action, shooting a hostage in the leg. Dillinger screamed at Nelson to hold his fire as the Buick careened out of town.

The posse of Police Chief E.J. Patton could have closed in, but Patton hung back for fear of precipitating a fire fight with the bank robbers that could have resulted in the massacre of the hostages. Eventually, Patton let the gang slip away. Dillinger released the hostages, and the gang made good its getaway.

In need of medical attention for wounds they had suffered at Mason City, Dillinger and Hamilton made for St. Paul, Minnesota. Hamilton brooded that he should have shot the cashier, Fisher, in Mason City, who Hamilton now realized had deprived him of $200,000. With characteristic bravado, Dillinger, Hamilton, and Homer Van Meter barged into the office of Dr. N.G. Mortenson, the St. Paul Health Officer. While Van Meter menaced him with a sub machine gun, Dr. Mortenson dressed and bandaged the wounds Dillinger and Hamilton had suffered. Homer Van Meter apparently threatened his wife and children, and menaced Dr. Mortenson; the doctor never did reveal the unscheduled appointment with the Dillinger gang until years after the fact.

The gang then dispersed for a time, with Dillinger and Billie Frechette taking an apartment at the Lincoln Court Apartments in St. Paul.

Dillinger continued to work on a plan to break Handsome Harry Pierpont out of the Ohio State Penitentiary. Pierpont was guarded round the clock by prison guards reinforced both by federal agents, and the Ohio National Guard. Knowing that getting to Pierpont would be difficult, Dillinger passed the word to friends in Chicago that he needed detailed information on the exact circumstances of Pierpont's incarceration.

Somewhere along the line Dillinger's whereabouts was leaked to federal agents, who immediately moved in on his apartment in St. Paul. On the evening of **March 31, 1934**, agents R. L. Nails, and R. C. Coulter climbed the steps to the Lincoln Court apartment. Billie Frechette answered their knock, and, smelling trouble, put off the agents, telling them that her husband was asleep and that she was not dressed. Billie then re-locked the door and ran through the apartment alerting Dillinger, who dressed, grabbed a sub machine gun, and vaulted down the back stairs.

As agents Nalis and Coulter pondered their next move before the apartment front door, the unsuspecting Homer Van Meter walked into the building and began climbing the stairs in their direction. Challenged by the FBI agents, Van Meter nervously explained that he was a door to door soap salesman. Agent Coulter asked to see his samples, and Van Meter told him that he had left them in his car. Van Meter did an about face to find his samples, with agent Coulter close behind.

On the walk, Van Meter was able to pull his pistol and cover Coulter, who then ducked back into the building before Van Meter could fire. With no time to get into his car, Homer Van Meter did the next best thing commandeering a horse drawn delivery wagon, and whipping the horses down the street, in a helter skelter gallop away from the policemen.

While Van Meter made good his escape, Dillinger ran past FBI agent Cummings who had staked out the back alley. As Dillinger flew past him, Cummings snapped off a shot that tore through Dillinger's leg. But Dillinger's luck held.

He reached his Hudson Teraplane and roared out of the alley and into the street where he made good his escape before the federal agents could organize their pursuit. Dillinger had business in Chicago, but before leaving St. Paul he passed the word to his men that they would rendezvous in Mercer, Wisconsin, at the Little Bohemia resort hotel, then in the off season, and hopefully deserted.

Little Bohemia came highly recommended by Dillinger's pals in Chicago. It was owned by Emil Wanatka, who had retired to Wisconsin after a long and colorful career as the proprietor of a speakeasy in Chicago that had been the favored watering hole for sports figures, politicians, and gangsters alike.

While Dillinger was enroute to Chicago, federal agents received a tip that he would visit a doctor in the Starks building in Louisville, Kentucky to get his leg wound taken care of. J. Edgar Hoover approved a major FBI stake out and scores of federal agents and local police surrounded the building awaiting the arrival of the famous patient. Even while the stakeout was in progress the story was leaked to the Herald Post, which published the story in the afternoon edition under the banner headline, "U.S. Lays Dillinger Trap Around Starks Building." John Dillinger never did keep that appointment, and J. Edgar Hoover and company took another beating in the press for having again missed the elusive bank robber.

In Chicago, Dillinger's first stop was at Jimmy Probasco's place, the veterinarian turned surgeon to the mob, for work on his leg wound. Then Dillinger visited the office of his attorney Louis Piquett. Dillinger passed Piquett a bundle of green backs for laundering, and Piquett assured him that when the time came his financial arrangements would be in order. Piquett then relayed a message that Frank Nitti would be at Wrigley Field that afternoon.

Dillinger attended the game, the opener of an early season series between St. Louis and the Cubs, in which Dizzy Dean and Lon Warneke, the "Arkansas Humming bird", were the opposing pitchers. Sporting his Mex disguise, Dillinger made his way to the row of seats behind Nitti's box on the first base side near the Cub's dugout. Nitti, seemingly engrossed in the game, casually reached back and handed Dillinger a note. The note stated that arrangements with Jimmy Lawrence were in place, and that the "outfit" required another delivery of goods from Dillinger. Dillinger said only "okay", before moving to another vantage point to watch the remainder of the game.

In the first week in **April, 1934**, Dillinger returned to Mooresville to visit his family. The bank robber made no effort to hide his presence, and on one afternoon he openly visited the local newspaper to read the stories that had been written about his exploits. There were visits with friends and Dillinger finally turned up at his family home in Mooresville, Indiana, where he shared a Sunday chicken dinner with Billie Frechette and his father.

When questioned later about his reunion with his son, the senior Dillinger explained, "Oh, yes, John came down here to look in on me. He was hurt in the leg a little, but not much. I don't aim to tell no lies, even to keep things like that quiet. I didn't tell the police because they didn't ask me. John's not in Indiana now."

Dillinger had detoured to the Ohio State Penitentiary in the hope that he could still devise a plan to free Handsome Harry Pierpont. The Penitentiary was an armed camp, and Dillinger reluctantly gave up his plan to shoot his way in to free Pierpont. The Indianapolis Star had a field day with Dillinger's brazen "Sunday dinner" with his family, right under the noses of policemen who supposedly had staked out the family home.

The Commissioner of Public Safety complained, "It's mighty queer that people would tell a newspaper about Dillinger's visit before they told police or other law enforcement agencies." While police agencies moved to seal off Mooresville, Dillinger escaped the cordon with Homer Van Meter; and on **April 12, 1934**, the pair looted the armory at Warsaw, Indiana.

Dillinger and Van Meter delivered their take in weapons to the Kostur Hotel in East Chicago before beginning their drive to the Little Bohemia resort in Wisconsin.

On **April 13, 1934**, Clyde Barrow, the Texas bank robber and murderer, pushed Dillinger off the front pages with his celebrated letter to Henry Ford. Barrow boasted that he always stole a Ford V-8 for his getaways, so powerful and reliable were the automobiles. Writing from Tulsa on April 10, 1934, Barrow positively eulogized the big Fords to their maker. "While I still have got breath in my lungs I will tell you what a dandy car you make. I have drove Fords exclusively when I could get away with one. For sustained speed and freedom from trouble the Ford has got every other car skinned and even if my business hasn't been strictly legal it don't hurt anything to tell you what a fine car you got in the V-8."

Only weeks before, on the afternoon of March 31, 1934, Clyde Barrow and his lethal consort, Bonnie Parker, had been a hundred yards off the road between Grapevine and Roanoke in North Texas when two highway patrolmen literally stumbled upon them. Bonnie and Clyde shot first and never did ask any questions. As one policeman writhed in agony in the dust, Bonnie dispatched him with two shotgun blasts that exploded the man's head like an over-ripe turnip.

To John Dillinger, Bonnie and Clyde were plainly and simply two-bit killers. Clyde Barrow's public letter to Henry Ford, and the publicity it generated, prompted the Indiana bank robber to call an impromptu press conference in which Dillinger called the Texas killers "trigger happy amateurs" who were "giving decent bank robbers a bad name." Dillinger had given the press yet another scoop, and law enforcement officials again with egg on their faces doubled their efforts to locate the bank robber and put him down.

Even in late April, the sprawling two story log and clapboard Little Bohemia Lodge, at the top of Wisconsin, was still snowed in. By **April 20, 1934**, Dillinger and Van Meter were reunited at Little Bohemia with Jack Hamilton, and Baby Face Nelson. The heat was on, and the gang intended to lay low for a few weeks. Dillinger clearly was preoccupied, prowling the Lodge through the cold nights and spending hours listening to the radio in the main ballroom, and staring at an old band poster for Bix Beiderbecke and his Wolverines.

In the middle of one night, Van Meter walked in and quipped, "That trumpet player's been dead since 31." Dillinger smiled, "Maybe so, but if you listen up real good, you can still pick up the echoes." "Sure you can, Johnny, sure you can," said Van Meter, as he made his exit. Johnny Dillinger grinned wryly, and stared into his not altogether settled future, "hearing" the golden, burnished tones of the legendary Bix, and feeling just then the melancholy mood that lingered on at Little Bohemia. Dillinger's moment of reverie would be short lived.

In Rhinelander the phone rang in the FBI office, and the tipster tersely announced, "If you want Dillinger, get up to Little Bohemia." Earlier that day, Emil Wanatka's wife, Nan, apparently tired of the guests who had essentially taken over the Lodge, absented herself to visit family. In a fit of anger, she may have made that call, to the everlasting regret of her husband.

The agent immediately relayed the information to the office of J. Edgar Hoover in Washington, D.C. Hoover contacted Melvin Purvis, the agent in charge in Chicago, and instructed him to travel immediately to Little Bohemia, saying, "take him alive if you can, but protect yourself."

Attorney General Cummings made no bones about his expectations. "Shoot to kill - then count to ten." Mel Purvis assembled a group of FBI agents, and Indiana State policemen, and flew into Rhinelander, where he met another group of agents who had driven in from St. Paul. Reinforced, the Purvis group set out for Little Bohemia in four cars. The going was rough over the snow covered roads, and enroute, two of the cars broke down. The displaced agents rode the running boards of the remaining two cars as Purvis pushed on.

At Little Bohemia, the agents moved away from their cars and covered the last hundred yards through the pines and snow drifts on foot, with only the beams of handheld flashlights showing them the way. With his men in place near the front entrance, Purvis was about to order another group around back when three men walked out of the darkened Lodge, and made for a car parked out front.

Without warning the agents opened fire, cutting down the three strangers, none of whom had anything to do with the Dillinger gang. A Civilian Conservation Corps worker was killed, a CCC cook, and a gas station attendant, wounded.

Alerted by the gunfire in front of the building, Dillinger and his gang were able to escape out the back before Purvis could react to seal off their escape. Baby Face Nelson, who had been in a bungalow out back with his wife Helen, stayed behind as a rear guard, trading machine gun bursts with the agents, before he too melted away into the night. Purvis's men continued firing into the Lodge throughout the night. In the icy morning silence, Purvis entered the all but demolished Lodge only to find it deserted, except for the hotel staff, and the Dillinger gun molls who had hidden in the basement to escape the fusillade.

Little Bohemia was a fiasco for the FBI, in fact, and in the press. The bank robbers had again eluded the FBI dragnet. Even the international press carried the story. An editorial in the London Express stated, "Hull said a few words yesterday about Wall Street, which will help you understand the atmosphere of the country in which Dillinger works. When a community lets a pack of man-eating tigers dwell in its midst, it is easy for a lone wolf like Dillinger to slip under the fold gate . . . . Capone had got that business down to a fine art.

Nobody has followed him because conditions have been changed. In the present confusion of the economic crisis it is the lone raider type you would expect to flourish. Hence "Dillinger." The humorist, Will Rogers, commented, "Republicans coming out pretty strong now against administration. Looks like if the Democrats don't get Dillinger they may lose this fall's election."

Prior to "Little Bohemia", FBI jurisdiction was severely limited, and included only the Mann Act, interstate prostitution, the Lindbergh Law, interstate kidnapping, interstate auto theft, and "crimes against the United States." Although they were in fact armed to the teeth in the field, the letter of the law still prohibited the FBI agents from carrying weapons, and required that local police make all arrests, even in cases involving the FBI.

Clearly, the G-Men needed greatly expanded "powers" in the field to be able to successfully combat the depression era criminals. In the words of Attorney General Homer Cummings, "We are now engaged in a war that threatens the safety of our country - a war with the organized forces of crime."

On **May 18, 1934**, Congress passed six new laws and gave the FBI the "teeth" it needed to end the depression crime wave. For the first time it became a federal crime to kill or assault a federal agent, or to cross state lines to avoid prosecution. The "extortion" of money by telephone, or any other interstate instrumentality, became a federal crime, and, most importantly, the robbery of any bank that was a member of the Federal Reserve System was likewise a federal crime.

Finally, FBI agents were authorized to carry guns, and make their own arrests. In the flush of his greatly expanded powers, J. Edgar Hoover immediately took the offensive against John Dillinger, imposing a shoot to kill order. The U.S. Government placed a $10,000 reward on Dillinger's head. So too did five States in the mid-west.

Over the next two months there was a mass hysteria in the chase to find John Dillinger, as some half dozen look a likes were arrested, some narrowly escaping police bullets. In early May, Chicago police were convinced Dillinger had escaped to England. Scotland Yard was alerted to check all vessels coming in from Canada and the United States. The search narrowed to one vessel in particular, the Duchess of York, out of Halifax. A meticulous search failed to turn up the American bank robber who was then rumored to have slipped through the police cordon to make connections with the London underworld.

Bonnie and Clyde death car.

On **May 23, 1934**, the law enforcement community regained a measure of its self-respect when the Texas Rangers and local police caught up with Clyde Barrow and Bonnie Parker in a quiet corner of Louisiana, chopping them to pieces from ambush with automatic weapons and small arms fire.

Only the end of Bonnie and Clyde, their wakes and funerals in Dallas three days later, and the Barney Ross - Jimmy McLarnin fight on **May 30, 1934** at the new Long Island bowl, moved John Dillinger off the front pages, and then only for a day.

Time Magazine published a parody of a new board game, called "Dillinger Land". On the board, the game began at Crown Point, Indiana. After tracking Dillinger through the mid-west, and each of his alleged bank jobs, the board stated "Game Ends Where?" The Board then declared, "Here 5,000 Federal agents, sheriffs, deputies, posses, constables, and Indians, were covering all possible trails from Little Bohemia."

Finally there was the cryptic declaration, "On top of last 'X' will lie John Dillinger, corpse." But would he? The Nation held its breath, watching and waiting, their feelings ambivalent toward the bank robber who had captured their imagination in taking down the banks that many of them believed had caused the great depression.

In the last week in June, Dillinger's sister, Mrs. Audrey Hancock, took out a notice in the Classified ads of the Indianapolis papers extending birthday greetings, "My darling brother, John Dillinger, on his 31st birthday. Wherever he may be, I hope he reads this message." John Dillinger's father was invited to join the local vaudeville circuit as a speaker, and, on at least two occasions, the old man did speak publicly, displaying a certain backhanded affection for his son and while still condemning his illegal acts.

A petition for amnesty was begun in Mooresville, Indiana, in much the same way as amnesty had been granted to the legendary Frank James some sixty years before. The petition to Indiana Governor McNutt explained, "We find precedent in the case of Governor Crittenden's pardon of Frank James in the state of Missouri, in which case James became a useful and respectable citizen of the state until his death."

The petition continued, "John Dillinger has never manifested a vicious, revengeful or bloodthirsty disposition, there being considerable doubt as to whether he has ever committed a murder. It is our belief that Dillinger fell into the wrong channel of life in his youth, from which escape is almost impossible, and that if given the above opportunity he would gladly avail himself of it and live up to it."

Reporters from the local citizenry continued to feel a kind of defiant affection for their notorious native son. A gas station attendant told one reporter that he "liked Dillinger fine," and a Mooresville banker admitted to a writer that Dillinger had been seen openly visiting with his old friends in Mooresville. Shocked that Dillinger's presence had not been reported, the writer asked, "You mean to say that the most wanted criminal in America could stroll around here in his home town, 18 miles from Indianapolis, without anybody turning him in?" The banker flatly replied, "Nobody ever did!"

Billy Frechette, still in police custody, disclosed a snap shot of the reconstructed Jimmy Lawrence that was duly entered into police records as a picture of John Dillinger by unsuspecting officials. On **June 30, 1934**, at 11:30 a.m., a withdrawal of $25,000 was made at gunpoint from the Merchant's National Bank in South Bend, Indiana. The owner of a nearby jewelry shop ran into the street during the robbery and swore that he had fired a shot at Baby Face Nelson, a shot deflected by Nelson's bullet proof vest.

After the robbery, hostages were taken and forced to ride the gang's running boards until they were finally set free on the west side of South Bend. Hostages on running boards had the look of a Danger job, but eyewitnesses weren't so sure. Some swore that Dillinger had been there. Others said that none of the faces matched any of Dillinger's gang.

There were reports that Nelson had been spotted in the far west, apparently on the "lamm" to his previous home in Southern California. There was a persistent rumor that Dillinger had been seen near El Paso, Texas. But how could these sightings be accurate if the Dillinger gang had in fact just robbed a bank in South Bend, Indiana? The public outcry grew, "Where was Johnny Dillinger?"

Chapter 8

The Biograph

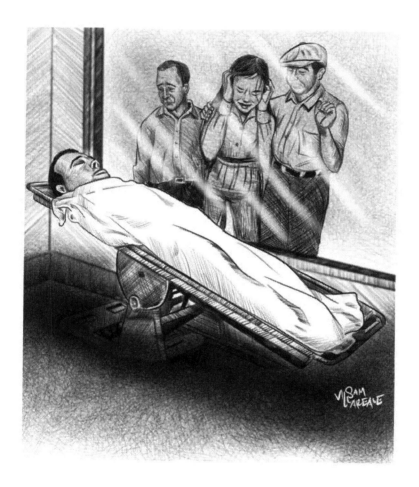

The Aftermath: Myth or Mystery?

The Biograph
The Aftermath: Myth or Mystery?

Fourth of July weekend, Chicago, 1934. Jimmy Lawrence was in the back room at the Bucket of Blood speakeasy when a pair of East Chicago cops entered the barroom. Introducing themselves as detectives Wright and Larsen, the East Chicago policemen told the sweeper that they needed to talk to Jimmy Lawrence. The old man leaned on his broom and answered that Jimmy Lawrence hadn't been around much lately, and then asked, "But if I should see him, what can I tell him it's all about?" Wright tersely snapped, "Tell yer pal it's about South Bend, understand, be sure you tell him, South Bend!"

Jimmy Lawrence's ear had been glued to the door, and as the detectives left the speakeasy, Lawrence stepped into the barroom. The sweeper was about to speak, but Lawrence cut him off, saying, "I know, I know." Lawrence sought out his girlfriend, Polly Hamilton, and confided what he had over-heard. Lawrence had pulled the Merchants National Bank job in South Bend the prior week with Sergeant Zarkovich and a crew from the East Chicago precinct.

Nitti's boys had guaranteed there would be no heat. Lawrence protested, "What's going on?" Polly Hamilton assured Lawrence, "It's nothing, don't worry about it," but as soon as Lawrence left, Polly placed a call to a secret "emergency" number she had been given. The man on the other end never identified himself, and said only, "What do you have?" Polly reported the conversation with Lawrence and the visit by the East Chicago detectives. The man said, "Okay. It'll be taken care of."

Within the hour, Sergeant Martin Zarkovich had been briefed on the actions of detectives Wright and Larsen. Both had been nosing around Zarkovich's operation, and apparently were working alone to expose the renegade group in their own police department that was pulling the Dillinger 'look-a-like' bank jobs. Zarkovich moved swiftly to put an end to it.

In the early morning hours of **July 5, 1934**, detectives Wright and Larsen were found shot dead, gangland execution style, in the Chicago stockyards. The papers identified them as dirty cops, probably on the "outfits" payroll, who had double crossed their mob bosses and paid the price. What they knew about Jimmy Lawrence and the Dillinger 'look-a-like' bank jobs died with them.

On **July 12, 1934**, a meeting was held in the office of attorney Louis Piquett. Polly Hamilton attended with Anna Sage, the madam who ran the East Chicago houses of prostitution for the Chicago "outfit". Willie Bioff would later also attend the meeting. The Immigration and Naturalization Service had gotten on to the fact that Anna Sage was in the United States illegally. The Service threatened Anna Sage with deportation to her native Romania, unless she immediately began cooperating with local police in a drive to break the Chicago prostitution rackets.

Piquett advised Anna Sage that her alien status could be taken care of if she agreed to play a part in a little deal being worked out by the Chicago "outfit". Anna Sage, desperate to avoid deportation, was easily enlisted in the mob's plan. Willie Bioff finally arrived at the meeting in Louis Piquett's office, an hour late. Bioff, known for his brutality with "working girls", was admitted to the scheme in order to keep the women in line, should they later falter or think better of performing their parts exactly as instructed.

Piquett outlined the plan. Friendly East Chicago cops would contact local police agencies to tip them to the appearance of Jimmy Lawrence at some public place. The East Chicago police would be present when Lawrence showed, but would muddle up the stake out to ensure that he escaped, with the local police on his tail, believing that he was Dillinger. At that point, the "outfit" would help Jimmy Lawrence disappear into lucrative retirement, permanently.

When asked by Polly Hamilton what would happen if there's shooting, Piquett replied, "Jimmy Lawrence will take his chances just like the rest of us if something goes wrong. There's a lot of dough in it for him if he gets away, and for his friends, Polly, even if he doesn't. All he's got to do is keep his mouth shut. Just like the rest of you — understand?"

One week later, **July 19, 1934**, Sergeant Martin Zarkovich of the East Chicago, Indiana police department, visited Captain John Stege, the officer in charge of the City of Chicago "get-Dillinger" squad. Zarkovich told Stege that he had a reliable tip on the whereabouts of John Dillinger in the next several days.

Zarkovich would hand the Chicago Police Department John Dillinger on a silver platter, provided only that they agreed to shoot the bank robber as soon as he appeared. Captain John Stege refused the deal out of hand, saying that even John Dillinger deserved a warning and opportunity to surrender.

Rebuffed, but not without options, Sergeant Martin Zarkovich's next stop was the Chicago office of the FBI. There Zarkovich met with agent-in-charge, Sam Cowley. Cowley, like John Stege, refused Zarkovich's shoot first and ask questions later' terms, but did agree that Zarkovich and his Captain, Timothy O'Neill, could spearhead the FBI stake out when Dillinger was exposed. Zarkovich assured Cowley that he'd receive word of Dillinger's whereabouts in the next day or two. Cowley alerted his immediate superior, Melvin Purvis. Purvis quickly approved the unorthodox joint FBI, East Chicago, and Indiana police department operation to get Dillinger.

J. Edgar Hoover was then briefed on the plan, and the Director, too, after voicing misgivings about Zarkovich, gave into his anxiety to be rid of the Indiana bank robber, whatever the price, and approved the plan. All that remained ˉwas to learn "when" and "where".

On the morning of **July 21, 1934,** Anna Sage entered the Chicago office of FBI agent-in-charge, Samuel Cowley, and there met with Melvin Purvis and Cowley. Anna Sage reiterated her concern that the Immigration and Naturalization Service continued to threaten her with deportation. Melvin Purvis promised her that, provided she cooperated with the law, she would never be compelled to leave the country. Her fears again quieted, Anna Sage delivered the message the FBI agents had been waiting for. Sage advised the agents that she would be attending a movie at the Marbro, or the Biograph Theatre in downtown Chicago the following night with John Dillinger. In order to assist the agents in picking her and Dillinger out of the crowd, Anna Sage stated that she would be wearing something in "red".

By 9 p.m. on the evening of **July 22, 1934**, the Marbro had been eliminated, and the FBI stake out was in place around the Biograph Theatre on Lincoln Avenue in the Loop. Sergeant Martin Zarkovich, and Captain Timothy O'Neill of the East Chicago police, watched and waited from their vantage point in Goetz's County Club bar, next door to the theatre.

In a room above the biograph, French Napier, a Loop bookie, manned his phones, taking action on the Cubs, as usual, but also kept an open line to Frank Nitti, who was an interested spectator in absentia at the Biograph that night.

It was a sultry night in the Loop, the air not moving, with pedestrians flocking to bars and soda fountains for liquid refreshments from the heat. A blue banner strung across the front of the Biograph proclaimed that the theatre had "Iced Fresh Air", and was "Cooled by Refrigeration". That primitive air conditioning, as well as the first run feature, Manhattan Melodrama, starring Clark Gable, William Powell, and Myrna Loy drew a large crowd for the late showing of the film. As the time ran down past 10 p.m., FBI agents nervously mopped their brows in the heat and watched for the first sign that the film was letting out.

Only minutes shy of 10:30 p.m., the first spectators emerged from the Biograph. Quickly the sidewalks were crowded with the movie-goers who had packed the Biograph for the late show. Neither Anna Sage, nor John Dillinger was spotted. At 10:30 p.m., the 'woman in red' pushed through the front doors of the Biograph, into the night. Guns drawn, fingers tensed on triggers, the agents watched as Anna Sage, Polly Hamilton, and John Dillinger walked arm in arm out of the Biograph.

Seconds away from calling out Dillinger, Melvin Purvis was suddenly frozen by the pair of men running from Goetz's Country Club toward the Danger party. Zarkovich and O'Neill charged at Dillinger, their guns drawn. Dillinger wheeled, recognized them, and strangely did not immediately flee. Some second sense then

propelled Dillinger to flight, but too late. Martin Zarkovich coolly came up behind Dillinger and fired into his neck and back.
Shot dead, Dillinger dropped to the pavement.

The FBI contingent quickly ringed the death scene. Zarkovich proclaimed that he'd shot Dillinger in self-defense. None of
the agents had seen the bank robber draw a gun. Zarkovich knelt
beside the corpse, and turning it, came out with a .38 cal. revolv-
er that had been underneath Dillinger. Zarkovich and O'Neill then
melted into the crowd.

Eyewitness accounts "strangely" were at odds with the
"official" version of what occurred that night at the Biograph. A
mechanic standing in front of his garage, directly across the street
from the theatre, witnessed the shooting. "Suddenly I saw a tall
man fire two shots in quick succession. He seemed to be standing
almost beside the man who was shot. The wounded man fell to the
alley without uttering a sound."

A woman who watched the shooting from the window of her
second story parlor backed up the mechanic. "I thought at first that
it was a holdup and the victim was killed." But FBI communiques
made no mention of the East Chicago police presence at the Biograph that night.

**Crowd after John Dillinger was ambushed at the Bio-
graph Theatre.**

A reporter from the Indianapolis Star brought the news to the elder Dillinger on the farm in Mooresville. Barefoot, in his farmers' garb of overalls and work shirt, the old man was dazed at first, stammering, "Is it - true? Are - you really sure there is no mistake?" Assured that there had been no mistake, Dillinger's father said "Well - well, John is dead. At last it has happened - the thing I have prayed and prayed would not happen." The old man wept, but slowly his manner changed as the circumstances of his son's death sunk in. Dillinger's father finally incensed, saying somberly, "They shot him down in cold blood." When given the news, Dillinger's sister Audrey broke down and cried, "He was just like a son to me."

The National Press initially abandoned its former bank robbing "darling", declaring that FBI agents had finally caught up with John Dillinger in a shoot out outside the Biograph Theatre in Chicago. The Cleveland Plain Dealer reported that Dillinger's former cohorts, Handsome Harry Pierpont and Charlie Makley, then residents of Ohio's "death row", would not be told of Dillinger's death. Prison officials believed that keeping Pierpont and Makley "in the dark", would continue their hope that Dillinger would bust them out of prison, and minimize the possibility that they might attempt their own escape from the "inside".

Melvin Purvis took credit for "beating Dillinger to the draw". J. Edgar Hoover said in Washington, D.C., "Justice had been done," but strangely, the Director had words of praise only for Sam Cowley, commending his "persistence, patience and energy that made it possible for the Division of Investigation to attain this success . . . ."

Above the Biograph, French Napier whispered into the phone line to Frank Nitti, "It's done, boss!"

"John Dillinger Was Dead", so said the FBI, and every newspaper running the story. Melvin Purvis became an instant media hero as the man who took Dillinger down, keeping his boss, J. Edgar Hoover, and his fledgling FBI out of the headlines. Purvis couldn't have known it then, but Hoover mentally drew a line through his name, striking his name from the list of active FBI agents. Purvis would shortly be "retired" because his boss believed either the "agency" or its "director" should have the headlines.

Moreover, Hoover, staunchly committed to the mythology of scientific crime fighting that he had created for his FBI, immediately began reconstructing history. For years Hoover would say that finger prints found in Sheriff Holley's car when Dillinger broke out of Crown Point ultimately lead to his capture, not betrayal by "the Lady in Red."

And what of the late John Dillinger? His body was taken directly from the walk outside the Biograph to the Medical Examiner's morgue in downtown Chicago. In his pockets were only a set of keys, $7.70, and a watch containing a snapshot of Polly Hamilton. Dillinger's sister, Audrey, was driven in from Mooresville to identify the baby brother she had raised.

Audrey came in with family friends. The family friends stared, squinted, gawked, and creased their brows during the morgue viewing. Some of them said it really didn't look like Johnny. Officials chimed in that the "years" had taken their toll. With no show of emotion, and with the air of a woman in a hurry, Audrey took one look and said, "There's no question in my mind - just bury him."

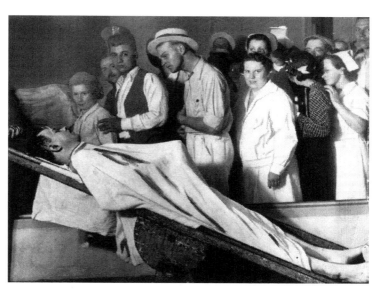

Two relatives of notorious 1930s gangster John Dillinger said they have "evidence" the body buried in an Indianapolis cemetery may not be him and that FBI agents possibly killed someone else in 1934.

Death photos in the morgue were compared to other available pictures of the late bank robber. Again there were similarities, but no certainty in the identification. A photograph of Dillinger with his girlfriend, Billie Frechette turned up. Of all the available pictures, officials agreed that one looked most like the corpse. Dr. Charles D. Parker, assistant to the coroner's pathologist, J.J. Kearns, performed most of the surgical autopsy.

John Dillinger was known to have gray-blue eyes. The deceased Dillinger had brown eyes. Dillinger had a mole between his eyes, and a scar on his lip. The deceased Dillinger had neither feature, but did have his top right incisor tooth, a tooth that never came in for the bank robber. Curiously, the deceased Dillinger did not have arm, shoulder, and leg scars that John Dillinger was known to have acquired in his many shoot outs with policemen.

Officials explained away those differences with "plastic surgery". But then the corpse seemed to have features that Dillinger didn't, a tattoo on the right forearm, black hair, rather than brown, and arching eyebrows, rather than bushy straight ones. Perhaps the strangest discrepancy was discovered in the comparison of John Dillinger's Navy physical some 12 years earlier, with the autopsy report.

The deceased Dillinger had a rheumatic heart in an advanced state of deterioration, John Dillinger's Navy physical never disclosed any evidence of a rheumatic heart condition, a condition that would have been thoroughly inconsistent with the physically demanding life style of the bank robber, beginning with his baseball playing years, and continuing through his 'athletic' escapades in robbing banks, from leaps over teller railings, to foot chases and shoot outs. Finger print identification was inconclusive. That one was attributed to scarring that probably resulted when the bank robber attempted to obscure his prints with an acid scrape.

None of it seemed to matter. The "official inquest" was hastily convened, and just as quickly "concluded." The Associated press complained, "The man who ran him down was not present; the man whose bullet killed him was not named, and the informant who led him to his death was not mentioned." Within a week the autopsy report would "disappear" before finally turning up nearly 30 years later.

A group of mortician students somehow persuaded guards to give them a few minutes alone with the body in the morgue. A death mask was cast, and eventually it became the focal point, with the bank robber's trademark "straw boater", of the "Dillinger" exhibit in the ante room of J. Edgar Hoover's Washington office.

There were "doubts" and there were "questions", but, after all, it was Chicago, where "certainty" was sometimes uniquely defined. The FBI said it was John Danger, and for all intents and purposes the case would be closed for decades.

John Dillinger's "poor" father came to Chicago to claim his son's body, proclaiming that he had no money to bury his son. A visit to the office of attorney Charles Piquett changed all of that, and Dillinger's father took his son home to Mooresville, Indiana for a proper Christian wake and burial. The wake was held at the E.F. Harvey Funeral Home, and later the body was moved to the home of the bank robber's sister Audrey in Maywood for further "viewing". Thousands of friends and curious strangers filed past the casket.

The burial took place on a rise at the Crown Hill Cemetery in Indianapolis on the following Wednesday. The cemetery that provided the final resting place for President Benjamin Harrison, R. J. Galling, the inventor of the first machine-gun, and novelist Booth Tarkington now received its native son, John Dillinger. Prayers were recited as a flash thunderstorm hammered at the cemetery grounds. Even as the grave diggers began shoveling in the excavated dirt, mourners who had attended the wake were still muttering that "it sure hadn't looked like John Dillinger in that coffin."

A few days later, John Danger's "penniless" father had the casket uncovered and re-entombed under tons of steel and concrete. Rest in peace John Dillinger?

* * *

It was the week before **Labor Day, 1934,** when the mustachio'd "Mex" with the curly hair showed up again in East Chicago, Indiana. It was after hours, and the Mex walked slowly down the alley behind the Kostur Hotel. He melted into the shadows when three men suddenly emerged from a basement door carrying a rolled rug. They cursed to a man as they wrestled the rug atop a mound of trash, and the Mex heard one say, "That Bioff is crazy. This is too much." One of his companions cautioned, "Shut up. You know he's a sick bastard. It could be one of us next time!" The third man said, "Come on, let's wait inside, the truck won't be here for at least a half hour. She ain't goin' nowhere."

The trio re-entered the basement, and the Mex watched and waited, hearing only the plaintive cry of a train whistle far distant in the night, and his own harsh breathing. The Mex moved to the rug, touched it, and recoiled at the wet. He knew he should leave it alone, but his curiosity had the better of him. Besides, the mention of Willie Bioff, a man he disliked, made certain that he would take a look. The Mex pulled at the rug, unrolling it. Even in the shadows, its grisly contents were almost too much to take. It was a woman, a young woman, cut in half at the torso, her face slashed at each corner of her mouth, fixing her expression in death in a grotesque grimace.

"Leave it be, my son," said the voice behind the Mex. Frank Nitti had entered the alley from the far end entrance to the Bucket of Blood speakeasy. His bodyguard, Louis "Little New York" Campagna, and another man were with him. Frank Nitti gestured nonchalantly back at his men. "You know "Little New York". He watches me." Nitti chuckled, pointing at the other man. "That's young Jack Rubinstein. The kid wants to be a fighter. So we took him on for odd jobs. He watches "Little New York." The Mex's expression betrayed his apprehensions. Nitti turned to Campagna, pointed at the rug, and said "Take care of that, will you," and gestured for the Mex to follow him out of the alley.

"Forget it my son, forget it," said Nitti, who then handed over a list of bank accounts and numbers, each in a different Mexican bank. "Christ, Frank," said the Mex, "The man's a monster. How can you?" Nitti cut him off, "It's none of your business, Johnny boy. Understand!"

Nitti's tone softened, "Besides, dead men on their way to sunny Mexico can't talk anyway, can they?" He pocketed the account summaries. They totaled more than a quarter million dollars, his ticket to a second life. He said, "Goodbye, Frank," turned, and walked out of the alley, never looking back.

Before year end, 1934, St. Paul police pumped 50 bullets into Homer Van Meter, unceremoniously sending him to meet his maker. In **October of 1934**, Melvin Purvis caught up with Pretty Boy Floyd in an open crop field in Ohio, and cut him down with a burst of sub machine gun fire.

That same month, 'Handsome Harry' Pierpont was strapped into the electric chair, his reward for the cold blooded murder of Sheriff Jess Sarber. At peace with himself, Pierpont smiled at the gallery and said, "Today I am the only man who knows the who's and how's and as my end comes very shortly, I take this little story with me."

In **November of 1934**, Agent Sam Cowley and another agent caught up with Baby Face Nelson. Traveling with his wife Helen, Nelson and his pal, John Paul Chase, could have driven off, losing the FBI men. But Nelson swaggered out of the car, firing his Thompson sub-machine gun as he came, and walked straight into a hail of lead laid down by the FBI men who had taken cover in a road side ditch. When the guns went silent, Sam Cowley lay mortally wounded, his fellow agent, dead. Baby Face Nelson turned and walked back to his car. He sat beside his wife, complaining that he had been hit; and didn't feel well. In minutes he was dead, riddled by 17 bullets from the guns of the FBI agents he had taken with him.

Martin Zarkovich attempted to collect an Indiana reward on the "head" of John Dillinger. Governor McNutt coldly turned down Zarkovich, saying, "It is a sordid picture." Zarkovich eventually became the Chief of Detectives in East Chicago, Indiana, and finally, the Chief of Police. Zarkovich was always known as a hard case, and a close mouthed man.

Matt Leach, the tenacious "stuttering" Indiana State policeman who dogged Dillinger throughout his career, bitterly complained that the FBI distorted what really happened at the Biograph on July 22, 1934. Leach knew that Dillinger had been shot by the East Chicago policemen, and not federal agents. For the balance of his Indiana police career, Leach made it a policy never to cooperate with the FBI.

Finally, on **Sept. 4, 1937**, J. Edgar Hoover succeeded in persuading Leach's boss to ask for the garrulous policeman's resignation. Leach spent the next several years preparing a manuscript that he asserted would tell the real story of what happened to John Dillinger. Matt Leach and his wife were killed in an automobile accident on the Pennsylvania Turnpike while returning from a conference in New York City with a publisher. Matt Leach's book was never completed, and his revelations died with him.

Polly Hamilton worked for room service at the Ambassador East Hotel, providing "services" not on the menu, until suddenly she came into an inheritance that permitted her to retire to a fancy Gold Coast apartment. Polly died of tongue cancer in 1969.

Melvin Purvis was unable to keep his promise to Anna Sage, the "lady in red". Anna Sage was deported to Romania in 1938. There she became a cabaret entertainer, on more than one occasion bitterly complaining that some day she'd return to the United States to tell the whole story.

After going on stage one evening and telling the audience that she would soon be telling the truth about John Dillinger, Anna Sage was found dead at roadside in Romania in April of 1947. Her death went into the books as an unsolved homicide, but one Romanian policeman who said "she lived too much in the past" might not have been far wrong.

Melvin Purvis

Melvin Purvis expected to eventually become assistant director of the FBI to J. Edgar Hoover. Instead, and to his surprise, Hoover secretly stage managed his resignation. Purvis then embarked on a career in Hollywood as a writer of G-Man pulps and films. His career always seemed on the verge of taking off, but never quite got off the ground. Purvis never knew that his former boss, and friend, J. Edgar Hoover, sabotaged every significant opportunity Purvis ever had in show business.

In 1961, Purvis learned something that terribly disturbed him. He walked to his gun case, and removed the .46 cal. automatic with which he was said to have shot and killed John Dillinger. Purvis placed the weapon in his mouth and blew his brains out.

Willie Bioff was sent to Hollywood by Frank Nitti to help Bugsy Siegel run the west coast rackets, and to begin union and studio shake-downs. Willie Bioff hooked up with George Browne, another displaced soldier from the Chicago "outfit", and together, Bioff and Browne succeeded in extorting millions of dollars from a number of major studios, principally Joe Schenck's Twentieth Century Fox studio.

Schenck finally went to the police and testified against Bioff and Browne. Both were convicted after trial, but by 1943 Bioff decided to "talk" his way out of prison. His testimony resulted in extortion and racketeering charges being brought against Frank Nitti and most of his lieutenants in Chicago.

By 1943 Nitti was in poor health, his chronic bad stomach mushrooming into respiratory and heart problems. The prospect of a protracted prosecution, and probable incarceration, plunged Frank Nitti into a life threatening depression. When the indictments were handed down a drunk was seen staggering along side the railroad tracks in Riverside, near Chicago. Passersby jeered at him, and the drunk pulled a gun and fired wildly at them. He then placed the pistol to his temple and pulled the trigger. Frank "the Enforcer" Nitti would never stand trial again, at least not in this world.

Frank Nitti, Boss of the Chicago Mafia, was found dead alongside the railroad tracks in Riverside, near Chicago. He died of a self inflicted gun shot wound.

Out of the rackets by the 50's, Willie Bioff changed his name to Bill Nelson and retired to the desert outside of Las Vegas. There he gardened, working particularly hard on his flowering hedge of lantana and plumbago. He also did odd jobs at Vegas casinos, brokered cattle, and dabbled in diamonds. Mostly, though, he postured himself to friends as a retired businessman, played the retiree and curried the favor of up and coming politicians, loaning Barry Goldwater the use of his plane and services as a pilot.

In November of 1955 Bill Nelson waved goodbye to his wife, and walked to his Ford pick-up truck to make the drive into Vegas. The explosion blew Bill Nelson's body some 25 feet from the wrecked truck. His wife, in shock, said of Nelson, "He was so good and kind. He didn't have an enemy in the world." The murder of Willie Bioff remains unsolved.

Crime scene photo of Willie Bioff's car after it exploded killing him instantly.

Louis Piquett, Chicago's counsellor to the "rich and infamous", eventually got himself indicted with his investigator and two physicians for fabricating evidence. After trial Piquett was acquitted, the jury buying his defense that he was only trying to help a client. Years later, Piquett finally got himself into a mess too deep for his adept footwork, and he was disbarred. But even that misfortune was temporary as Governor McNutt eventually pardoned him, and Louis Piquett returned to the practice of law.

Years of living on the fence, temporary legal setbacks to the contrary notwithstanding, had been quite lucrative, and Piquett retired to a life of leisure and, as one friend put it, "contentment". Jimmy Probasco, the "outfits" money launderer and sometimes plastic surgeon, offended the wrong person and was dropped head first from a 19th story window in downtown Chicago.

J. Edgar Hoover remained the first and only director of the Federal Bureau of Investigation until his death at the age of 77. Basically a bureaucrat, and a terribly effective one at that, Hoover did on occasion venture forth to perform as a line agent, more for the image of the agency, than any innate urge to be a street cop. Hoover personally took then public enemy #1, Alvin Karpis, and also accepted the surrender of Murder Incorporated boss, Lepke Buchalter.

But through the years Hoover remained primarily committed to ridding the country of subversives and communists, an ambition which he pursued with diabolical efficiency for decades, to the apparent exclusion of many other avenues of legitimate, and perhaps needed, agency inquiry. To some extent, with the passing years, Hoover became something of law unto himself, defying even Presidents to take him down a peg.

When Lyndon Johnson occupied the oval office he was expected to fire the venerable Director. Johnson, however, kept Hoover on, explaining that it was better to have him pissing inside the barn, rather than on it from the outside. Hoover made many enemies among the politicos of the times, but none were able to take him on or take him down.

It was said that the Director had a secret dossier on just about anybody in America that amounted to anything, and the secrets in his files were more than enough to insulate him from any attacks. In his old age, Hoover, increasingly the "anachronism" and "curmudgeon", spent an embarrassing amount of time talking about the good old days when his agents took down John Dillinger. In the Director's eyes it had been the crowning achievement that put his FBI on the map.

After his son's "death," John Dillinger Sr. appeared "on stage. In person, with members of his family" in many theatres in the mid-west, so strong was the popular sentiment to keep the Dillinger legend alive in the retelling of his exploits. John Dillinger's father was nearly 80 when he died in 1943. The father was buried next to his son at the Crown Hill cemetery. Dillinger's older sister, Audrey M. Dillinger Hancock, lived to the ripe old age of 98 before dying in her sleep on March 30, 1987 in Indianapolis, Indiana. She was said to have often reminisced about her baby brother Johnny, and "whatever had become of him."

The Mex remained south of the border for more than ten years before finally settling in Southern California, where he did odd jobs under the alias "Johnny Black". The "Mex" was in Los Angeles in January, 1947. At 7:30 a.m. on a sunny morning, on Jan. 18, 1947, a little girl was being walked to school through a vacant lot by her mother. They stumbled upon the nude body of a young woman, her torso bisected at the waist, the corners of her mouth sliced into a macabre grin. The Mex had seen another women similarly slaughtered years before. The Mex spent years on his own time attempting to identify the killer. Along the way, his path again crossed that of Willie Bioff, and the Chicago "outfit". The case came to be known as "The Black Dahlia".

Despite his success in forging a new life, the Mex was a troubled man, confiding in his one close friend that he had bought out by letting another man be led to the slaughter. The Mex never explained just what exactly happened. Over the years the Mex developed a reputation for tracking missing persons. On one occasion the flamboyant west coast gangster, Mickey Cohen, hired the Mex to track down a lady friend of his, Juanita Dale Phillips, who Cohen believed was being unlawfully "detained" in Texas.

It turned out that Juanita Dale Phillips was the famous stripper, Candy Barr, and that her detention was actually a lawful arrest by the Texas Rangers on a Marijuana charge. More importantly, the Mex learned that Candy Barr's troubles stemmed from a blackmail scheme hatched by some of his old acquaintances in Chicago, who had forced Candy to star in a porno film shot at a Texas motel. One of Frank Nitti's bodyguards, a kid named Jack Rubinstein, whom the Mex had met in the alley behind the Bucket of Blood in East Chicago, was involved. By that time the bodyguard was living in Dallas and had changed his name to Jack Ruby, but that is another story.

Chapter 9

New Directions After Prohibition

New Directions After Prohibition

Stephano Magaddino

While depression bank robbers grabbed the headlines, the "national" mob quietly got its house in order. Stephano Magaddino returned to the Niagara Frontier to stabilize his personal situation. There were liquor distributorships, a taxi company, cement and construction jobs, gambling, and illegal alcohol.

In the United States, Magaddino's territory began on the Niagara Frontier, with Buffalo and Niagara Falls, and included the Ohio Valley to Youngstown in the west; northern Pennsylvania, Pittstown, Scranton and Wilkes Barre; and in central and eastern upstate New York, Rochester, Syracuse, and Utica. In Canada, Hamilton and Toronto answered to Magaddino, and his tentacles reached even into Montreal, the key point of entry for his smuggling routes.

These were tranquil days for Magaddino's upstate criminal empire. Joe DeCarlo ran the territory west of Buffalo, including Erie and the Ohio Valley. Russell Bufalino would eventually oversee all of northern Pennsylvania. The Falcones answered to Magaddino from Utica, and there was a "working relationship" with John Sebastian LaRocca in Pittsburg.

Legitimate businesses were fronted by John C. Montana. Magaddino was shrewd and intelligent, using violence sparingly, but ruthlessly and decisively, when necessary. He was revered as "Don Stephano" by his underlings, a tribute to his old country roots, and he ran a tight spartan operation, permitting "real money" to trickle from the top only as and when necessary to insure the loyalty of his "soldiers."

It was the **Spring of 1932** when Stephano Magaddino drove to Cleveland to meet with Johnny Scalish, the Cleveland boss, and Lucky Luciano. Charlie Lucky came up from New York City with Joe Adonis and Frank Costello from the Broadway mob to discuss the liquor smuggling operations. There had been minor hijackings along the various routes, but the mob had quickly eliminated the foolish interlopers. Toronto was kept in line by the Volpe brothers, loyal lieutenants. Montreal had been more difficult to keep in the fold, but business there was now also running smoothly. Magaddino knew that Charlie Lucky could have used the phone, or sent someone to speak for him. Maggadino was certain that liquor convoys and hijacking weren't the only things on Luciano's mind that day in Cleveland.

Magaddino had worked with Maranzano in the former bosses lucrative immigrant smuggling business. Both men retained "connections" in Sicily, and were able to insure security at the point of departure. In fact, Magaddino had personally gone back to the old country after Maranzano's death for a homecoming of sorts, where he rekindled family connections that had lain dormant since his immigration. Magaddino's attention to detail paid off. Some 3,000 of his countrymen had entered illegally over a three year period, many of them earmarked for service as "soldiers" in Maranzano's organization.

Charlie Lucky asked Magaddino whether his "contacts" in Sicily were "still good". "Certainly," replied Magaddino, who, thinking one step ahead, asked himself, "To what purpose?" Then Luciano inquired, "How is business going in Montreal?" Magaddino controlled the mob family in Montreal, an appendage of the Corsican mafia, known as the "Unione Corse". As the pivotal point of entry in the international smuggling route into the Great Lakes ports, Magaddino had for years cultivated his Montreal connections.

Magaddino explained that his Montreal connections were "as good as gold", and then Luciano made a telling observation. "I hear the Corsicans and the Greeks are at each others throats over "dope". Magaddino was not unaware of what was happening in the Mediterranean. Narcotics smuggling had for some time been the private monopoly of the brothers George and Elias Eliopoulos. From their base in the Levantine areas of Greece, the Eliopoulos brothers bought up the Turkish opium crops, refined them into saleable drugs, and sold them to gangsters in

America, including Lepke Buchalter, and Dutch Schultz. The Corsican boss of the Marseille underworld, Paul Carbone, was moving in on The Greeks. Carbone and his underbosses, Stefani and Foata, were old acquaintances of Magaddino. It was this Corsican Crime family that controlled Montreal, and did business with Magaddino.

Magaddino eyed Luciano and observed simply, "Carbone's boys are gonna' have it all." Neither mob boss could know it quite then but they were speaking about what would one day be known as "The French Connection", a narcotics "operation" that began in Turkey, and proceeded to refineries in Marseille, and then moved finished product into the United States.

Luciano concluded the conversation by saying, "You know, Steve, prohibition ain't gonna' last forever." Magaddino was mildly shocked. Luciano had done time for narcotics possession years before, and was a vehement opponent of mob involvement in big time narcotics. The penalties simply were too stiff. Magaddino personally opposed dope dealing. It was "dirty business", better left to others in the criminal brotherhood. But millions of dollars in profits were being generated in smuggling by the Corsicans, and independent gangsters in the United States.

Was Luciano signaling one of his famous "about faces", an unanticipated move into another area of rich profits? Magaddino left the meeting unsure of Luciano's intentions, but with the resolve that his "Montreal-Great Lakes" smuggling route would be security tight for the moment when Luciano might change its business from liquor to "darker" goods.

* *

The Province of Quebec, Canada, and its first city, Montreal, were in the thirties in many ways anachronisms. The predominantly French speaking population desired both political and economic independence from Ottawa, and indeed, the British Empire, generally.

They had gained neither. In fact, the English minority, in alliance with interests in the United States, owned and directed the major economic enterprises of the Province. Railroads, banks, and insurance companies were directed from Montreal. Canadian-American conglomerates controlled the hydro-electric and related wood pulp industries, as well as the burgeoning Montreal-Est. petroleum refineries. And Montreal was the center for the great distilleries of John Molson.

The worldwide Depression seemed to pass lightly over the province of Quebec. The Provincial government gave economic interests free rein with a laissez faire policy reminiscent of conditions in the United States beginning some 50 years before and at the end of the 19th Century. Through it all, the Quebecois, the French speaking Roman Catholic majority, suffered silently.

Politically alienated, victimized economically, the Quebecois waited on a provincial political "turn" that would finally give them their due, and begin to "separate" French speaking Canada from Ottawa and the Commonwealth. Maurice Duplessis was to be their savior. A Conservative, who became the leader of the new Union Nationale Party, Duplessis was the odds-on favorite to win power in the Province by the mid-thirties.

Maurice Duplessis believed in free enterprise, in its broadest sense. Any economic venture, even one with a foot on the wrong side of the law, had a chance to survive if the return was sufficiently lucrative. Social and political reforms were paid lip service, but little else would happen to change the status quo.

Stephano Magaddino was not unacquainted with Duplessis. Each had interests in the giant distilleries of Montreal and Quebec. Duplessis fostered a "look the other way" environment, which permitted the American liquor smugglers to cut profitable deals with their Canadian distillery partners. Magaddino looked after the relationship at the top in terms of the broad principles of the agreement and the dollar split. He met with Duplessis at the Place Jacques-Cartier, in the Vieux-Montreal "old city." Duplessis welcomed continued "cooperation" with the esteemed businessmen from Buffalo. There had, by that subtle gesture, been a meeting of the minds and little else was said between them. The remainder of their time was devoted to the social amenities.

Magaddino left the day-to-day supervision of his Quebec interests to Giuseppe Tangone, a recent emigre from Sicily. Tangone was barely in his twenties, yet he was already a "qualified man" in the secret society. Tangone had narrowly escaped Mussolini's agents by sailing to Corsica. From there he illegally entered the south of France where he spent a year in Marseille, working for the Corsican mob bosses who had aided him in his escape.

His "route" to America took him through the great Harland and Wolff shipyards on Belfast Lough, in Northern Ireland. There, Tangone worked for six months and saw the Great Depression squeeze the life out of Belfast shipbuilding. The yards originally employed 20,000 workers, but the international economic calamity forced the cancellation of most orders, and not a single new vessel was launched from the Harland and Wolff yards in 1932 and 1933. When Tangone arrived, the labor force in the yards was down to 2,000.

Their gravely deteriorating economic situation drove many workers to violence in the streets. Many of Tangone's co-workers became involved in the street riots against fascist thugs known as "Blueshirts." Tangone had witnessed much of the same thing in Italy with Mussolini's "Blackshirts." He joined the rioting with the Irish friends not so much from political conviction, but rather because drawing the blood of "Blueshirts" was to him simply another "swing" at the hated Mussolini.

Although his original destination was New York City, Tangone learned from his new friends in Belfast that thousands of dock workers had immigrated to Quebec and found employment on the docks in Montreal. Tangone joined a group of workers leaving for Montreal, and entered Canada in 1934. He quickly established himself as an "expediter" on the liquor smuggling routes into Buffalo, and in short order became a trusted lieutenant of the Buffalo Don in Montreal. By this time also, his name had been anglicized to "Joe Tango."

Tango was ideally situated to see to the Don's business in Montreal with his connections to the Corsican mob and the recent Italian and Irish immigrants who worked on the docks. His facility with the French language made it possible to quickly establish himself with the French Canadian politicians and policemen who would have to be dealt with. So sure was Tango of his "connections" that he guaranteed to Magaddino that he could hold "open" Montreal as necessary to do the mob's bidding. Magaddino took Tango at his word, and sent a message to Luciano that the Canadian connections were in place and would remain so for the foreseeable future.

Chapter 10

Luciano Runs out of Luck

The Mob Turns West,
Fascist Friends, and Murder Inc.

Luciano Runs out of Luck, The Mob Turns West, Fascist Friends, and Murder Inc.

By the end of 1935, most of the mob's well known independent bosses had been taken off the board. Legs Diamond was killed in an Albany rooming house in 1931. On Feb. 8, 1932, Vincent "Mad Dog" Coll was gunned down in a Harlem phone booth in what was the final "act" of his insurgency against former boss, Dutch Schultz.

In May, 1932, Al Capone began serving an 11 year term for tax evasion. In December of 1933, Waxy Gordon was put away for 10 years on tax evasion charges. With Capone and Gordon in jail, the IRS turned its attention to the flamboyant Dutch Schultz.

Twice Schultz was tried for what the government believed were air tight tax evasion charges. In **April of 1935**, a jury in Syracuse could not reach a decision, and Schultz was spared by virtue of a hung jury. The government quickly an-

Following Al Capones incarceration, Dutch Shultz (left) became the next target of the IRS.

nounced that he would be retried, this time in the "north county," in Malone. Schultz quickly took up "residence" in Malone and spread a lot of money around getting acquainted with the locals.

While Schultz awaited trial, his pals in New York, convinced that the Dutchman would surely be convicted the second time around, began to cut up his territory. Aided by Schultz' trusted bookkeeper, Abraham "Bo" Weinberg and New Jersey boss, Abner "Longy" Zwillman, they moved in on many of Schultz' operations.

Charlie Luciano got wind of what was happening and decided on a "hands off" attitude until the issue was settled between Schultz and the IRS. The word passed to Zwillman to go easy and the status quo was maintained.

Schultz' retrial took place in Malone, New York, in **July of 1935**. The government had no difficulty establishing that Schultz indeed had received hundreds of thousands of dollars in undeclared income. The attorneys for Schultz did not contest the government's proof, but rather admitted receipt of the income, with the defense that since it had been generated by unlawful enterprise, "gambling," it was not subject to income tax. The jury returned with the completely unanticipated verdict of "not guilty," and Schultz was quickly on his way back to New York.

Schultz was angered by the partial dismantling of his operation, but Longy Zwillman was too highly placed to be "taken out," and Schultz settled for the head of the bookkeeper who had betrayed him. Bo Weinberg was murdered and dumped with "cement shoes" into the East River. The headlines Schultz had made in his battles with the IRS now made him "Public Enemy #1."

Special Prosecutor Tom Dewey focused the full force of his office on Schultz. Soon, the word was out that Dewey had "turned" witnesses who would testify that Schultz personally murdered an upstart associate in an Albany Restaurant in March of 1935. Schultz had in fact killed Jules Modgilewsky at that time and place. As Dewey's investigators closed in, Schultz began coming apart. The Dutchman could deal with the prospect of a jail term, but the electric chair was another matter.

Schultz, in desperation, passed the word that there was a $100,000, "open contract" on Dewey. Lucky Luciano moved quickly to deal with Schultz. Schultz' fate was discussed in Luciano's 39th floor suite in the Waldorf Towers. Frank Costello, Meyer Lansky, Bugsy Siegel, Joe Adonis, and Stephano Magaddino were in attendance. There was no question in any of the bosses' minds that it was bad business to kill a cop or prosecutor. But Luciano was faced with a dilemma.

The publicity craving independent bosses who operated under his wing had for years diverted attention from his very existence.

Luciano personally kept a very low profile, living under the pseudonym "Charles Ross" in the Waldorf Tower. But now all of them, "Mad Dog" Coll, Legs Diamond, Capone, and Waxy Gordon were gone, and Dutch Schultz was about to be. Luciano knew that he then would be Tom Dewey's prime "target." Luciano probed for another way out, but his assembled under bosses were unanimous in agreeing that there was no choice but to deal with Schultz. Luciano made it unanimous. Dutch Schultz had to go.

On the evening of **Oct. 23, 1935**, Dutch Schultz dined with some of his boys in the back room of the Palace Chop House and Tavern in Newark. Surrounded by Abe Landau, Bernard "Lulu" Rosenkrantz and Otto "Abbadaba" Berman, Schultz railed against Tom Dewey. After dinner Schultz excused himself to visit the "men's room."

Dutch Schultz disobeyed a direct order from the Commission and was murdered on Oct. 23, 1935 by Lucky Luciano's hit team, Murder Inc. members Charles Workman and Mendy Weiss, acting on orders from Lepke Buchalter. He was shot in the bathroom, but staggered out and sat down at a table and died.

At that moment, Luciano's hit team entered the restaurant. Schultz was shot where he stood in the men's room. His pals were murdered where they sat at the table. Schultz, mortally wounded, lasted into the next day and expired in a babble of incoherence's without fingering his killers.

Tom Dewey, right, was a special prosecutor in New York with 72 successful prosecutions of organized crime cases. Following the death of Dutch Shultz, Dewey turned his energy towards Lucky Luciano, undisputed kingpin of organized crime in New York City.

Tom Dewey

With the Dutchman barely in the grave, Tom Dewey declared war on Lucky Luciano. Dewey publicly proclaimed Luciano New York City's "overload of vice," accusing him of presiding over a $10,000,000 a year prostitution ring, which employed some 200 "madams," and 1,000 "working girls," all of whom paid Luciano "tribute." Dewey worked secretly to "turn" some of the women against Luciano, and soon there were whispers heard, even on the 39th floor of the Waldorf Tower, that Dewey indeed had succeeded in convincing some of the girls to testify against Charlie Lucky.

Luciano certainly was the kingpin of organized crime in New York City, but he was stung by the accusations that he personally called the shots for a vice empire that operated on the proceeds of prostitution. Underlings might actually do the dirty work on the streets, but as "chairman of the board," Luciano saw his participation as remote, and, as such, sanitized. But Luciano was not about to take Tom Dewey lightly, however dubious he believed the "evidence" to be.

Midwinter, the end of the first month of 1936, and Luciano was "in hiding" at Owney Madden's resort spa at Hot Springs, Arkansas, to avoid Dewey's subpoenas. From Hot Springs, Luciano convened the key members of his syndicate to plot the organization's course in the coming years, with or without Charlie Lucky at its head. Frank Nitti came in from Chicago, Stephano Magaddino from Buffalo, and Frank Costello, Joe Adonis, Bugsy Siegel, and Meyer Lansky from New York, and its environs. The Anastasia brothers, Tony and Albert, were also included, as was Lepke Buchalter.

The Chicago "outfit" had for years controlled most criminal activity west of the Mississippi. The mob had sent George Browne and Willie Bioff to Los Angeles to begin infiltrating the film industry. Already, that pair had seized control of the International Alliance of Theatrical Stage Employees, for use in major studio shakedowns.

Now Luciano, with Nitti's cooperation, would send Bugsy Siegel west to take over all control of the mob's operations there. Las Vegas would come later. For openers it was Hollywood, and the gambling ships that plied the Baha and Southern California coastal waters. The Anastasia brothers and Lepke would continue their takeover of the docks, the Fulton Fish Market, and the garment industry.

The Longshoremen's Union was already captive. Inroads were also being made in the two major garment workers' unions. Meyer Lansky had designs on the Teamsters union, but significant penetration of that union would not occur until well into the forties.

Frank Costello and Joe Adonis would preside over the mob's gambling and restaurant business. Prohibition had been a bonanza for illicit liquor production and smuggling, but "repeal" had finally been approved. Costello argued that "legitimate" beer and liquor distributorship could replace the prohibition profits. To a certain extent they did, but an enormous vacuum, nonetheless, remained in the mob's business and profits.

Luciano had something "new" in mind. Narcotics had been the province of independent gangsters, some, but not all of whom paid tribute to the mob. Henceforth, and despite the obvious risks with law enforcement, and the continuing repugnance of narcotics to the senior mafiosi, Luciano's syndicate would control the major narcotics smuggling routes into the United States.

Stephano Magaddino's smuggling pipeline from Montreal to the Great Lakes ports of Buffalo and Cleveland, and to Detroit, would become the principal pathway into the country for narcotics from refineries in the south of France. Magaddino personally opposed narcotics, in much the same way as Luciano had distaste for prostitution.

Both were "dirty business." But both generated enormous profits, and someone would surely reap those revenues if the syndicate opted not to. Magaddino's reservations were rationalized. It was "smuggling," like it always had been, only white powder would now be in the "pipeline", not liquor, and god have mercy on the poor devils who got "hooked".

* * *

By **Spring of 1936**, indictments had been returned against Lucky Luciano in the "prostitution" investigation presided over by Tom Dewey, and Luciano was compelled to return to New York to face the music. The trial would begin in June, and Luciano signaled his bosses to make sure that security was tight on each of their operations.

Stephano Magaddino summoned Joe Tango from Montreal and discussed with him the situation in the port of entry for "the pipeline." Tango again assured Magaddino that his house was in order. Magaddino invited his brother-in-law, Nick Longo, into the meeting. Longo resided next door to the Don on Whiting Avenue in the Falls. He ran a gambling operation in Buffalo, and had been acting as Magaddino's liaison with Tango in Montreal, splitting his time between the two cities.

Longo had observed nothing that would cause him to question Tango's assessment of the situation. Everything was in place. All that remained was for Corsican boss Paul Carbone, in Marseille, to open "the tap" on his end from the refineries. In mid-May, Magaddino again met with Luciano, and assured him that everything was a "go" for business through "the pipeline."

The Whiting Avenue neighborhood in Niagara Falls was blacked out and "asleep" in the early morning hours of **May 19, 1936**. It was five in the morning when a knock sounded at the side door of Nick Longo's house. Nick was away in New York City and his wife, Arcangela, Stephano Magaddino's sister, sleepily padded through the house to open the door. Behind Arcangela fell in her three young daughters, who had been awakened by the commotion and were curious to see who was outside their door at so early an hour.

Arcangela opened the door and an explosive charge was triggered. She was killed instantly and her daughters were injured, but each eventually would recover.

Stephano Magaddino was both furious, and incredulous. What manner of "low life" would make "war" on an innocent woman and her children, regardless of the wrong? Nick Longo returned from New York City and faced a grim and relentless questioning from Magaddino. Longo finally admitted that he had double crossed his partners in a gambling venture. He was the intended target of the bomb.

Longo "fingered" the trio, and Magaddino summoned Joe Tango from Montreal, an unfamiliar face in Buffalo, to "take care of it." Tango did just that, the three disappeared, and Magaddino banished Longo in disgrace from ever returning to Buffalo. The Don then picked up the pieces of his dead sister's family, taking in her three daughters, and raising them as his own.

* * *

Lucky Luciano's trial began in **June of 1936**, and before the month was over a New York City jury returned a verdict of guilty against him. A sentence of 30 to 50 years, a severity previously unheard of in such cases, was swiftly imposed, and Luciano was taken to the Clinton Correctional Facility in Dannemora to begin serving his sentence.

In Luciano's absence, Frank Costello acted as a kind of "prime minister" for the mob, coordinating illicit activities across the country. Stephano Magaddino devoted his energies to the importation of Sicilian mafia apprentices, "picciotti", as the New York mafia families lifted their "on again-off again" ban on increases in membership. He was also involved in piecing together the largest sports betting "action layoff" network east of Chicago. In Rochester, the heavy action was taken by Luke Smith and Mikey Troy, in Utica by the Falcones, and in Cleveland by Johnny Scalish. What the Mob needed was access to a national wire service that would permit them to tie in the eastern gambling hub with Chicago-Kansas City, and the west. That's where Bugsy Siegel came in.

Siegel had been in Hollywood for three years, since 1936. Joe Epstein, the mega-buck Chicago bookie, had hit upon the idea of putting all the Mob gambling centers on line with a single wire service that not only would give them instant access to action and results, but also would permit the laying off of heavy bets anywhere in the country. Siegel was about other business, and Epstein signaled him to wrap things up so that the wire service deal could proceed.

George Browne and Willie Bioff were engaged in a studio shakedown at Warner Brothers, through their leverage with the stage-hand union. But Jack Warner would not pay. Browne hit upon an "object lesson" that would surely get Warner's attention, dropping a light fixture from atop a sound stage on James Cagney, who was starring with George Raft in the filming of "Each Dawn I Die". Raft got wind of the plot, and appealed to old pal Bugsy Siegel to put a stop to it. Siegel did just that, warning Browne and Bioff off and telling them that it was "bad for business" for them to even consider harming a hair on the head of one of America's great screen legends.

Hollywood business now in hand, Siegel turned his attention to the sports betting network. Johnny Scalish and Stephano Magaddino in the east signaled their consent to the deal. Joe Epstein, in Chicago, was its "architect." It remained for Siegel to "get to" Jimmy Ragen, the operator of the "Continental Press Service," to persuade him to enter into partnership with the mob bosses across the country. Neither promise nor threat could sway Ragen. He was an independent, and wanted to stay that way. Conversation exhausted, Siegel turned to enforcer Mickey Cohen to "reason" with Ragen.

Ragen took a fearful beating with baseball bats before finally agreeing to be bought out by Siegel. Even at that, Siegel was so enraged at Ragen's stubbornness that the wire service deal was closed over Ragen's dead body. Jimmy Ragen survived mob bullets, before finally succumbing to mercury poising in the hospital. Siegel transformed Continental into the Transamerica Wire Service, and the national mob gambling network was born.

In western New York, profits rolled into coffers of the Magaddino crime empire. Magaddino succeeded in cornering the "Golden Wedding" liquor franchise for a pal in Rochester. The Buffalo Don was a frequent visitor to Rochester, where close relatives resided on Ruhr Street. Antonio "the Czar" ran the Rochester rackets in those days under Magaddino's ever watchful eye.

Magaddino seldom dealt directly. John C. Montana was his "point man". Magaddino, even then, devoted most of his time to national mob business. But his hometown management style served him in good stead for decades, principally his uncanny knack for squeezing underlings for "his cut", and knowing the precise moment when the pressure should be relieved to give them breathing room, insuring their loyalty.

In 1937 Vito Genovese was forced to flee the country and went back to Italy due to impending criminal charges. Arriving with a $250,000 bribe, Genovese became fast friends with Benito Mussolini.

It was business as usual into 1938 until a bizarre set of circumstances seemed to accelerate Luciano's timetable for opening the tap on the importation of narcotics from the Mediterranean, to flow into the country through Magaddino's Montreal to Buffalo "pipeline." In 1937, Vito Genovese, a trusted Luciano lieutenant, was forced to flee the country to Italy in the face of pending criminal charges. Genovese, with well documented mafia roots, was fearful that the fascist regime would give him considerably less than a friendly welcome.

Vito Genovese

Literally with hat in hand, Genovese immediately sought out Count Galeazzo Ciano, Mussolini's son-in-law and trusted aide. Genovese handed Ciano a case containing $250,000 as a token of his "sincerity." Tension of the moment evaporated and Ciano, remembering that Genovese had an extensive background in the construction business, in addition to his criminal specialties, asked Genovese whether he could spare the time to act as a consultant to the government on certain construction projects. Genovese not only found the time, but also personally financed and supervised the construction of a factory for the fascists. Mussolini himself commended Genovese, and awarded him the title of "commendatore" for his "service" to the government. Mussolini was pleased with the newcomer's "spirit of cooperation."

There was, however, one other matter, a "sensitive" situation of personal importance, which he hoped Genovese could help him with. Carlo Tresca was the publisher of Il Martello, an Italian language weekly published in New York City. Tresca had for some time been writing scathing editorials critical of Mussolini and his policies. Mussolini was angered by Tresca's writing and embarrassed that any Italian could be so critical of him. Genovese promised to take care of the matter and within a month his stateside "friends" did just that. Carlo Tresca was shot to death on lower Fifth Avenue in New York City.

Genovese's relationship with the fascists had now progressed beyond the bounds of normal "graft." He was in every sense "in with them," even to the point of arranging murders. With Mussolini it was politics, pure and simple, and a monstrous ego constantly in need of adulation. Ciano, however, answered to a different drummer. Ciano perceived the opportunity to acquire great personal wealth in those turbulent times, with Genovese as the point man for any number of lucrative illegal activities. Genovese played Ciano perfectly, first getting him personally hooked on narcotics, and then enlisting him as his covert partner in a narcotics smuggling venture.

Genovese got the word back to Lucky Luciano. Luciano, with clout even in prison, "arranged" his temporary transfer from Dannemora in the north country, to Great Meadows, just north of Albany. Frank Costello visited with him there. There were two matters on the agenda. The first was Genovese and the narcotics

Frank Costello was known as the "prime minister." He was the mob's supreme political fixer.

pipeline. Costello reported that everyone was in place. "Product" would move from Turkey, via Italian port cities, to the refineries of Paul Carbone in Marseilles. From Marseilles, the refined heroin would be smuggled into the United States via the Montreal -Buffalo "pipeline." Luciano was anxious to hear what Costello had "arranged", concerning his early release from prison. Costello, the "prime minister," was the mob's supreme political fixer, and he had spared no expense spreading the mob's money around to secure Luciano's early release.

Costello believed the best strategy was to contribute heavily to the gubernatorial campaign of a candidate likely to return the political favor, if elected. Paradoxically, Tom Dewey, the very man who had successfully prosecuted Luciano, was now running for governor against Herbert Lehman. Luciano was skeptical that Dewey would ever play ball, even if mob money helped him reach the state house. Costello wasn't persuaded. Campaign contributions were arranged, and the mob awaited the outcome.

Tom Dewey lost the gubernatorial election to Herbert Lehman, and with that defeat went Luciano's first chance to do "some business" regarding his release. Luciano and his lieutenants, however, continued to seek out any situation or circumstance that would give them the opportunity to build good will with the government, which eventually could reach a level sufficient to open Luciano's cell door.

The fall of Louis 'Lepke' Buchalter became one such circumstance. With the murder of Dutch Schultz and the jailing of Al Capone and Luciano, Lepke had become America's 'public enemy #1.' It was Lepke who had raised garment district and bakery extortions to the fine art of contract killings. 'Murder Inc.' was his creation, and Albert Anastasia his mafia partner and protector. His "staff killers" included Abe Relas, Pittsburg Phil Strauss, Charlie the Bug Workman, Allie Tannenbaum, and Frank the Dasher Abbandando.

By 1937, Relas and Tannenbaum were in custody, and talking. Relas catalogued 200 murders around the country, all of them Lepke's handiwork. William O'Dwyer and Burton Turkus in the New York City DA's office openly declared war on Lepke. Special Prosecutor Tom Dewey promised to put Lepke away for "500 years." J. Edgar Hoover said the FBI wanted Lepke for his part in a $10,000,000 heroin deal. With pressure from every quarter, Lepke went into hiding, under the protection of Albert Anastasia.

Frank Costello visited Lucky Luciano in Dannemora and advised him that the government dearly wanted Lepke, and wouldn't forget any help they received from Charlie Lucky. Clearly Lepke had to go, but the problem was devising a method to feed him to the wolves without arousing the anger of Albert Anastasia. Lepke was willing to do some time with the "feds," but he would not come out of hiding to face Tom Dewey and the State charges that included murders that might place him in the death house. A deal was struck to have Lepke surrender to the "feds" and thus avoid a state prosecution. Walter Winchell, the famed columnist, personally acted as the intermediary in the negotiations for Lepke's surrender.

It was a sultry summer night in Manhattan on **Aug. 24, 1939**. Albert Anastasia picked his pal Lepke up at 101 3rd St., in Brooklyn, and drove him to Fifth Avenue and 28th St. There Lepke walked across the street to a parked car, driven by Walter Winchell. J. Edgar Hoover himself sat in the backseat and personally accepted Lepke's surrender.

Lepke entered his Federal plea and received a 14 year sentence for narcotics smuggling. Luciano scored points for stage managing Lepke's surrender. And finally, even Tom Dewey was satisfied as the "feds" turned Lepke over to the New York authorities to face the music on the murder charges. Lepke saw it as a double cross, but it all became academic. Admitted perjurers and killers made the state's case against Lepke.

The New York Court of Appeals on Lepke's final appeal deadlocked 3 to 3 on the issue whether the mob boss had received a fair trial. Chief Judge Herbert Lehman, casting the deciding vote, agreed with defense counsel that Lepke indeed had not received a fair trial, but then unaccountably ruled that the "error" was "harmless," and that the death sentence would be enforced.

Of course what Lehman had done, legal technicalities to the contrary notwithstanding was leave Lepke, the "monster" architect of Murder, Inc., to his fate. Lepke was electrocuted in Sing Sing on March 4, 1944. Abe Relas, the songbird who began Lepke's problems, received his reward on **Nov. 12, 1941** when he was thrown from a window in the Half Moon Hotel on Coney Island while in 'protective custody.'

On Nov. 12, 1941, Abe Relas was thrown out a window in the Half Moon Hotel on Coney Island while in 'protective custody.

The mob's narcotics business boomed briefly in 1938 and early 1939, before the tramp of the jackboots of Adolph Hitler's legions put Europe at war and effectively cut trade routes, both legal and illegal to America. Tom Dewey sought the Republican Presidential nomination in 1940, but again lost. The "mob minions" breathed a collective sigh of relief. They preferred Dewey in New York where he might do some good, if and when.

With the narcotics smuggling routes temporarily shut down, the mob turned to new endeavors of a domestic variety. Bugsy Siegel was now firmly entrenched in California. He and Frank Costello were convinced that a resort gambling hotel in Nevada, where gambling was legal, would be a bonanza for the mob. The location would be Las Vegas, a sleepy desert crossroads that was then clearly a distant second to Reno and Tahoe as points of interest for tourists in Nevada.

Thus began the saga of Bugsy Siegel and his Flamingo Hotel.

Chapter 11

The Flamingo Deal And Luciano's Pardon
Then Havana and Bugsy Siegel

The Flamingo Deal And Luciano's Pardon
Then Havana and Bugsy Siegel

The year was **1941**, the month of **June**, its **18th** day. Joe Louis was fighting Irish Billy Conn in the Polo grounds this night, and for a few hours America could push aside news of the widening war in Europe to tune its radios to "the fight." The mob was there, too, because Frank Costello and Meyer Lansky had shrewdly judged that this was the time to convene the bosses to determine who would take "points" in the Vegas deal. The bosses occupied a training room deep in the bowels of the Polo Grounds.

Preliminary fights were winding down, and the mobsters were anxious to conclude business so they could get to ringside seats for "the fight." Bugsy Siegel gave a glowing report as to what they could expect from his "Flamingo" hotel and casino. The construction budget was $1.2 million. Even with overruns, Siegel was confident the Flamingo could be built for less than $2.0 million.

Meyer Lansky declared that he and Bugsy would take 20 percent. Frank Costello said he and Charlie Lucky were in for 20 percent. Dandy Phil Kastel from New Orleans, took 10 percent, as did Tony Accardo for the Chicago outfit. Moe Dalitz from Cleveland, spoke for himself and the Magaddino family in Buffalo and took 10 percent. The remaining 30 percent was divided between the New York City bosses, and the New Jersey organization.

Business concluded, the bosses retired to ringside where Louis and Conn put on one of the best heavyweight brawls of all time. Billy Conn, The pride of Pittsburgh, danced and hit some more, and through 11 grueling rounds had built a solid lead on the "Brown Bomber." In round 12, Billy Conn went toe to toe with Joe Louis, ripping him with both hands; but at the bell, Louis was still on his feet. Between rounds, Conn's handlers told him to stay away from Louis. All Conn had to do was finish on his feet to win. Conn wasn't listening. He was as tough as nails.

As far as Irish Billy Conn was concerned, "Tough guy's didn't dance." He charged off his stool for round 13 to take Joe Louis out.

At ringside Bugsy Siegel screamed at Conn to keep away from Louis. Bugsy had $25,000 riding on Conn, and as Billy Conn slugged with Joe Louis, Siegel saw his bet slipping away. Louis finally connected with a picture perfect left hook, then a right-left combination, and the "Pride of Pittsburgh," Billy Conn, was down for the count. When Billy Conn just missed beating the count, Siegel cursed the dead game fighter, but then relented. Conn simply "had to do it". Siegel had some of the same "metal" and stubbornness in him. He, too, had to build his Flamingo, even if it killed him.

* * *

On **Dec. 7, 1941**, the Japanese bombed Pearl Harbor, and America was plunged head long into World War II. The mob quickly adapted to the new wartime austerity and regulations. Paulie Castellano, then an up and coming New York mafioso, organized a group of meat purveyors to beat the rationing system through black market sales. Ration stamps were counterfeited and the mob turned substantial profits, beating the system.

Joseph "Socks" Lanza, known to his pals as "Joe Zox", the semi literate ruler of the Fulton Fish Market, worked with Tough Tony Anastasio to control the Longshoremen Union, and continue lucrative dock shakedowns and hijackings. There were no 'strikes' or espionage, and any pilferage was mob sponsored and not directed at the war effort.

It was business as usual for the mob, albeit with some new wrinkles. While the mob jealously guarded its "cut" of the war time action, they also agreed to work with the government to keep the docks free of Nazi saboteurs. As far as the mob was concerned the Nazi's were "bums" who deserved to be exterminated. More importantly, it would be "bad for business" if they disrupted commerce on the docks.

It was almost in passing that Joe Zox mentioned to Frank Costello that naval intelligence officers were daily on the docks, voicing their concerns about security. The kernel of an idea took hold and Costello drove to the north country to visit Lucky Luciano in Dannemora. The strategy was simple.

The mob would make every effort to assist the government with shore security. There would be no quid pro quo, but the government should understand that anything they could do for Charlie Luciano would be "appreciated." Costello returned to New York City and signaled Joe Zox and Anastasio to cooperate with navy intelligence wherever possible. He also hit upon an idea to really hook the government into its unholy alliance with the mob on the docks.

The S.S. Normandie had been the pride of France's transatlantic cruise fleet before the war. The outbreak of hostilities found it berthed on Manhattan's west side. The government intended to convert the great liner into a troop carrier. Frank Costello had other plans for it.

On **Feb. 11, 1942**, the S. S. Normandie burst into flames, lighting for miles the blacked out skies over Manhattan. Naval Intelligence was in a panic. Government officials were convinced that the Normandie catastrophe signaled the beginning of a concerted Nazi effort to paralyze the New York City docks. Who better to insure that the Nazi's didn't have their way than the mob bosses who really controlled the docks, day and night.

Again, there was no deal concerning Luciano but this time around his circumstances were "mentioned," and the government agreed to do what it could, but with no guarantees, since Luciano's release remained a New York State matter. Now, however, Costello had their attention, and other circumstances intervened to speed the process.

It was the **summer of 1942**. Lucky Luciano was transferred from Dannemora to Great Meadows, and then to a prison in New York City. Naval Intelligence had contacted Joe Zox about new business. Joe Zox knew it was out of his league when they mentioned contacts in Sicily. Frank Costello took over and met with Lt. Commander Charles H. Haffenden of Naval intelligence. Meyer Lansky attended the meeting, and finally Lucky Luciano himself was brought in for subsequent meetings.

Allied forces would soon be in North Africa. Operation Torch was scheduled for **November of 1942**. After North Africa, the next Allied target would be Sicily.

Naval Intelligence wanted the Sicilian Mafia to clear the way for the allied invasion. The question was, could Luciano deliver? Although he said there would be no problem, Luciano had been 40 years away from Sicily. But there were others in his criminal organization with closer connections to the old country.

* * *

Mussolini's campaigns in Greece and East Africa had become disastrous defeats. Only German intervention in North Africa in the person of General Erwin Rommel and the Afrika Korps had saved the Italian "colonies" in Libya, and Tunisia. As the tide of battle turned against him, Mussolini lost faith in his closest advisors. Count Galeazzo Ciano was no longer "trusted". His friend and partner, Vito Genovese, was now a fugitive from fascist justice. Don Calo Vizzini, the senior Mafia Don in Sicily, gave Genovese sanctuary.

Lucky Luciano was aware of these circumstances and worked on a method to turn them to his advantage in his dealings with naval intelligence. Stephano Magaddino had the old country contacts to enlist the aide of Don Calo Vizzini in implementing Luciano's "deal" with the government. Messages were delivered by Magaddino to Don Calo through merchant seamen who first sailed to neutral Spanish ports, and then transferred to smugglers' boats for the perilous final leg of the voyage across the western Mediterranean, to Sicily.

Don Calo Vizzini was more than glad to "cooperate," since he viewed the prospect of a United States occupation as a far better atmosphere for rejuvenation of the Sicilian mafia than the repressive policies of the fascist regime. Vito Genovese was enlisted by Don Calo to help where he could, and Genovese did just that, telling local mafia bands that the banner of Luciano himself would fly from the turrets of allied tanks when they rolled off the beaches of Sicily.

By the **end of 1942,** the pot was boiling in New York City. Tom Dewey had been elected Governor of New York. The government's campaign to enlist the aid of the Mafia for the Sicilian invasion was now christened "Operation Underworld." Lt. Commander Charles H. Haffenden was working closely with Frank S. Hogan and Murry Gurfein, two former associates of Dewey in his prosecutor's office.

Luciano's interests were represented by Moses Polakoff, his lawyer, and by Meyer Lansky and Frank Costello. Stephano Magaddino operated behind the scenes, at Luciano's direction, to insure that Sicilian Mafiosi would indeed cooperate when allied troops hit the beaches. Final preparations were in place by mid 1943, as the invasion fleet was assembled in North African ports.

✻✻✻✻✻

Allied troops landed on Sicilian beaches on **July 9 and 10, 1943**. On **July 14, 1943**, an American plane flew over Villalba, the home village of Don Calo Vizzini, and dropped a yellow flag inscribed with the black letter "L." This was the pre-arranged signal for Don Cabo to rally mafia members to disrupt fascist communications, and organize peasants to support the invasion. There were other air drops, each delivering packets of replica banners of the original "Luciano" signal flag.

American tanks soon flew the yellow and black banners from their radio antennae. Don Calo himself rode on one of the lead tanks, clearing the way for the Allied advance. So too did Don Guiseppe Genco Russo, the mafia boss of an adjoining sector. There was tough fighting in Sicily for the Allies where German units rushing south were able to make blocking stands against them, but by and large the "naval intelligence-mafia" plan achieved its purpose.

Fascist units were not a real factor in the campaign. The people of Sicily supported the invasion. Within weeks, Palermo and Messina were taken and Sicily settled in for another occupation, this time American and British. The Allied occupation units soon repaid the mafia for its "cooperation", installing a number of mafia members as mayors of key occupied towns.

In the United States, Lucky Luciano bided his time, waiting to collect his "marker" from the United States government. There was a scare in 1944 when Tom Dewey, contrary to his public statements, made a run for President. The Mob held its breath, but Luciano stayed "Lucky," as Dewey came up short. Tom Dewey, the man who had put Luciano behind bars, would remain in Albany to preside over the details of his release.

On **May 7, 1945**, a Petition for Executive Clemency was filed with Dewey on Luciano's behalf. Dewey referred it to the State Parole Board, most of whom were his appointees. The Parole Board recommended Luciano's release. On **Jan. 3, 1946**, Tom Dewey approved Luciano's parole, stating that Luciano had performed certain unspecified services vital to his country's war effort.

Dewey also indicated that Luciano had served more than nine years on the conspiracy to commit prostitution charge, a term amounting to the maximum anyone had served on such a charge in Dewey's memory. However, Tom Dewey had one final surprise for Luciano. Charlie Lucky had figured again to take up residence in the Waldorf Towers, and pick up the management of mob business where he'd left off 10 years before.

Dewey conditioned Luciano's release on his deportation from the United States to his native Italy. Luciano knew better than to cry "wolf" at Dewey's double cross. The government had kept most of its bargain. Luciano had his freedom. Whether he could continue to coordinate American mob activity as an exile would remain to be seen.

Charles "Lucky" Luciano, right, handcuffed to Lt. Francis O'Hearn at the train station in Harmon, N.Y. on Jan. 9, 1946. Luciano was en route to Sing Sing prison in Ossining, N.Y., where he was sent, to wait for deportation to his native Italy. (AP Photo)

On **Feb. 9, 1946**, the mob's "who's who" convened for Luciano's "bon voyage" party. Meyer Lansky, Albert Anastasia, Joe Adonis, Tommy "Three Finger Brown" Lucchese, Frank Costello, Joe Profaci, Joe Bonanno, and Stephano Magaddino were all in attendance. As Immigration Officials escorted Luciano to the pier, they were greeted by lines of longshoremen, standing at attention, turned out by Tough Tony Anastasio to bid farewell to the departing "chairman of the board." Luciano set sail for Italy on the S. S. Laura Keene, promising to "return" by year end for an off shore mob convention in the Caribbean.

That evening, Stephano Magaddino dined with his cousin Joe Bonanno. Both men were well aware of their pivotal power on the mob commission with Luciano now relegated to the position of "board chairman" in absentia. Frank Costello would speak for Luciano, but it was the commission's conservative wing, Magaddino, Profaci and Bonanno, who would backstop the implementation of Charlie Lucky's policies.

Magaddino and Bonanno then adjourned to the Copacabana, where Bonanno's eldest son, Salvatore "Bill" Bonanno, joined them. Joe Bonanno saw the coming years as an invitation to greater power and economic success, and declared his intention to bring his son Bill along quickly as a mafia apprentice. Stephano Magaddino was not so sure that things would proceed as smoothly as Bonanno anticipated.

Lucky Luciano had been the cohesive force that held the mob together in the past 15 years, despite the fact that he'd spent almost 10 of those years behind bars. With Luciano thousands of miles away in Italy, Magaddino wondered whether the mob's "machinery" would function as smoothly as it had in the prior years.

* * *

If Lucky Luciano had any doubts about how the coming months and years would play out he never voiced them, but rather immediately plunged into mob business as soon as he was settled in Italy. Luciano's first stop was a courtesy call to Don Calo Vizzini in Palermo. Luciano thanked Don Calo for his "cooperation" in the war time events that preceded Luciano's release from prison. Don Calo promised support for any ventures

Luciano wished to orchestrate in the "old country." Next, Luciano looked up old pal Vito Genovese.

Genovese had an uncanny knack for survival. He had switched from fascist "collaborator" to "partisan" in the nick of time. By the time Luciano arrived, Genovese had become the official interpreter for Colonel Charles Poletti, the Allied Military Governor. Genovese wasted no time in transforming this position of trust into a base for illegal activity. In short order, Genovese became the kingpin of a gigantic black market ring operated from the supply base at Nolu. Medicines, cigarettes, liquor, clothing, wheat, and food were traded from Genovese's illicit commissary.

Vito Genovese was more than happy to cut Luciano in on his black market action. Luciano enlisted Genovese in his plans to again operate a smuggling ring to bring contraband into the United States via the Montreal-Buffalo pipeline. Don Calo Vizzini would also be involved in the Italian end of the operation. Details remained to be worked out, with the major decision being tabled until Luciano's mob convention at year end.

Lucky Luciano set sail for Havana in late **October, 1946**. Meyer Lansky had been Luciano's advance man, paving the way for his visit with Cuban President Grau San Martin, and former "strongman," Fulgencio Battista. By **mid November**, Luciano was comfortably settled into a suite at the Hotel Nacional, and a posh hacienda on Quinta Avenida. A steady stream of mob dignitaries passed through his doors, principal among them, Frank Costello and Meyer Lansky.

Fulgencio Batista, Thelma Lansky, Meyer Lansky; Jewish Syndicate boss, top financial and gambling operations advisor for the Italian Mafia in America and casino operations front man (Las Vegas, Cuba, Bahamas), Havana, Cuba.) ca. 1946.

Sinatra and the mob in Havana, 1946. Top row: Paul Castellano, Gregory De Palma, Frank Sinatra, Thomas Marson, Carlo Gambino, Jimmy Fratianno, Salvatore Spatola; bottom row: Joe Gambino, Richard Fusco.

Ground breaking for the Flamingo Hotel had taken place in January of 1945. But war time shortages of materials caused delays and cost overruns, and by **mid 1946** the Flamingo had already tripled its original $1.5 million construction budget. Bugsy Siegel repeatedly called his partners "back east" for more money to bail him out of dollar shortages.

The Del C. Webb firm, of Tucson, Arizona, was the general contractor. Their reputation was beyond reproach: With 'VJ' day in August of 1945, the rationing of materials came to an abrupt end. Yet the Flamingo continued to flounder, as Frank Costello and Dandy Phil Kastel answered Siegel's distress calls, and pumped millions into the project.

Virginia Hill

Bugsy Siegel's mob partners were not fools. Early on they suspected that not all of their dollars were going into the Flamingo. Agents of Lucky Luciano in Switzerland reported to him that Virginia Hill, Siegel's girlfriend, was making regular trips to a Swiss Bank. Luciano had built his mob empire on Frank Costello's ability to fix things, politically.

Cuban officials initially denied the reports. Luciano had handsomely padded their coffers and would continue to do so, in the future. His presence was clearly good for the "business" of government graft. But the United States was adamant in its insistence that Luciano be asked to leave. And American aid was indispensable to the continuation of the Cuban dictatorship. The clock was ticking down on Luciano's Havana "incursion".

Christmas week, Havana, 1946. Lucky Luciano had succeeded, at least temporarily, in foiling the attempts of the United States to have him ousted from Cuba. For the time being the Cuban government was backing his stay, arguing that he was a private citizen who had committed no crime in Cuba, and who was not wanted elsewhere.

The mob dignitaries assembled at the Hotel Nacional. First and foremost was their insistence that Bugsy Siegel had to go. Luciano was well aware of the fact that Siegel had double crossed big mob backers, and struck out on his own in Vegas and Hollywood. But Luciano also knew that he must have an independent, loyal, "enforcement" arm outside the Sicilian mob "families" if he was to be able to back his policy decrees from across the Atlantic.

Bugsy Siegel

Siegel had always answered to Meyer Lansky and Lucky Luciano, and to no one else. Lansky had met with Siegel and received his assurance that the skimmed money would be returned just as soon as the Flamingo could be opened. Luciano was inclined to give Siegel a second chance, for both of their goods. A loyal and feared Bugsy Siegel would be all the edge Luciano would need in keeping the mob families "in line" in the coming years.

Frank Costello backed Luciano's play, but argued that Siegel must show some good faith. What better way to convince his skeptical partners than by opening the Flamingo for the "New Year" and showing a profit. The message was flashed to Siegel, and Bugsy reluctantly agreed to the early opening and to deal with the other bosses. But equally important to Luciano had been Meyer Lansky's "brains" and shrewd business judgement, and Bugsy Siegel's sheer "nerve", and penchant for violence. Had anyone else double crossed him, Luciano's retribution would have been swift and final. But for Siegel, there would be something of a reprieve. Provided the mob commission agreed when they convened in December, Luciano was inclined to give Siegel the opportunity to open his hotel, early if necessary, and to get it profitable quickly so that the cost overruns could be repaid.

Reporter Robert Ruark was in Havana in the **Autumn of 1946**. So too were Frank Sinatra, Ernest Hemingway, and Humphrey Bogart. Sinatra was there to discuss an invitation to entertain on a periodic repeat basis at one of the casinos, maybe also to deliver for one of Chicago's Fischetti brothers a "suitcase" of green to a distinguished visitor from Italy.

Bogart was in town to hype the late Havana release of his film, To Have and Have Not, and to meet with John Huston to discuss a new film project tentatively titled "Key Largo," which was to go before the cameras in early 1948 on location in the Caribbean, and after completion of his current collaboration with John Huston, "The Treasure of the Sierra Madre." Ernest Hemingway lived in Havana and was wrestling with a story line that would obsess him until his dying day, a novel that he'd never complete, but which would nonetheless be brought out 25 years after his death in a severely edited version called "The Garden of Eden."

Robert Ruark was covering politics in Cuba, in particular the changing political fortunes of Fulgencio Battista. Ruark quickly stumbled on a story far juicier than the one he'd come for. The rumors were rampant that Lucky Luciano had slipped into Cuba to chair a mob convention. Ruark finally confirmed them when he personally spotted Luciano prowling a balcony at the Hotel Nacional. Ruark quickly penned a story that the deported Charlie Lucky had pulled a fast one on Uncle Sam to sit off shore and continue to pull the strings for the organization on the mainland. Diplomatic wires were quickly buzzing with a flood of messages from the State Department to the Cuban government that Luciano was an "undesirable" who must be required to leave Cuba immediately.

As the Havana "convention" continued, the mob took up the question of its post war involvement in narcotics smuggling. Shipping lanes were once again clear of hostile "men of war". Combatant nations were disarming and looking to domestic issues. The populace generally was in the post war "high" of catching up on the "living" that the long years of hostilities had postponed.

The Luciano-Magaddino "Great Lakes-St. Lawrence" smuggling routes were in place. So too were the required connections with *"growers"* in Turkey, and "refiners" in the south of France. The army had finally caught up with Vito Genovese's black marketing in Italy, but Vito had maneuvered his way stateside, there beating a murder rap.

Genovese was ready to head up Charley Lucky's operation whenever he signaled that the time was right. The Trafficante family in Florida was already working on an alternative smuggling route from South and Latin America. The apparatus was in place, coiled like a snake ready to strike, awaiting only the throwing of the "switch" that would open the flood gates.

Luciano began with a torrent of negatives. Narcotics unquestionably was "bad business." Enforcement of penalties was aggressive. Jail sentences had been severe for those who were caught. Luciano had personally tasted these perilous "waters," and did not wish to do so again. But again and again, the refrain sounded that the profits could be enormous, and were there for the taking. And if not the mob, then surely some other criminal entity would become involved.

The mob bosses were by no means unanimous in their endorsement of the narcotics venture. In fact, dissenting mafiosi were free to go their own way. But as the night wore on it was clear that the classic rationalization of criminal conduct was gradually eroding all "reluctance." The mob had not created the "itch" - the demand. They were merely providing the "means" for private citizens to "scratch" it, and the horrible consequences of decades of drug abuse would therefore not be on their heads. Luciano finally declared that his "family," the Luciano-Vito Genovese outfit, would engage in narcotics smuggling, with Vito Genovese calling the shots.

Frank Costello would speak for Luciano on all other aspects of mob business. Most of the other bosses fell into line, directly in street distribution, in participation in International smuggling, or in taking a territorial gratuity from independent gangsters in their areas who were involved in the narcotics trade; as, for example, the Chinese, south of Canal Street in Manhattan.

A final matter involving the New York City docks and Fulton fish market was brought before "the House." Joseph "Socks" Lanza's authority at the market was affirmed, as was that of Tough Tony Anastasio, with the Longshoremen. Luciano indicated that Frank Costello would speak for him in his "physical" absence, and, on that note, the mob convention was adjourned.

In private, Luciano met with Stephano Magaddino, Meyer Lansky, and Russell Bufalino. Bufalino, then a youthful Lieutenant in Magaddino's "family," would be "loaned" to Lansky to act as a casino and race track manager, and general overseer of mob activities in Havana. Luciano anticipated a lengthy stay in Havana, and Bufalino would also arrange a courier service to pass Luciano's directives to the mainland, and to Frank Costello in New York City.

Luciano would be disappointed in the duration of the hospitality of his Cuban hosts. Mounting pressure from the highest levels of the United States government would force him to leave Cuba in the first weeks of 1947. Charlie Lucky would attempt his Cuban "ploy" in Venezuela, but again the intervention of United States governmental officials, principally Harry Anslinger, the head of the Federal Drug Enforcement Agency, would force him to put "distance" between himself and the Americas. In short order, Luciano was compelled to return to Italy on the Turkish freighter, S. S. Balch, where he would remain for the rest of his life.

* * *

In Las Vegas, Bugsy Siegel worked feverishly on his holiday opening. Show business pals pitched in to entertain and to act as "greeters" for the throng of "suckers" that were expected to mob the Flamingo. Georgie Jessel was the master of ceremonies and George Raft, Sonny Tufts, Jimmy Durante, and Xavier Cugat's orchestra were on hand.

A fleet of Constellations was chartered at L.A. International to fly in the "show biz" jet setters for the gala opening. Siegel himself, decked out in a cut-a-way, and Virginia Hill, wearing a "flamingo" colored gown, posted themselves in the main foyer to usher in guests and well wishers.

But Bugsy Siegel's opening would not go off as planned. Severe rain and windstorms kept the planes on the ground in L.A. The suckers stayed home, and the Flamingo opening bombed. By the end of the first week in 1947, the action had picked up, but Siegel was in ever deeper trouble. The casino lost hundreds of thousands of dollars across the tables as lady luck smiled on the players. Never had Siegel seen a gambling house take a licking like his Flamingo did in those **first weeks of 1947**.

Meyer Lansky reported the fiasco to Lucky Luciano and Frank Costello. Siegel was ordered to close the casino and hotel, and to re-open in **March-April, 1947**, hopefully under better conditions. Bugsy Siegel again balked. The "edge" must return to the house, provided the doors stayed open. His partners would not relent, and Siegel toyed with a "personal" visit to old pal Lucky Luciano. Meyer Lansky finally persuaded Siegel to do as he was told, and the lights temporarily went out at the Flamingo.

The Flamingo did reopen, as planned, but the bad run of luck continued. Again, his partners called for Siegel's head, and Luciano scrambled to save him. Finally, by **May 1947**, the Flamingo was solidly in the black to the tune of $300,000. It would stay that way for the next 30 years, earning millions for its mob owners.

In early June, Virginia Hill visited Europe, going first to Switzerland and then stopping in Paris. Now that money was again flowing for Siegel in Vegas, he was back to his old tricks, skimming from his mob partners. Luciano washed his hands of the situation. Siegel knew the mob had marked him for death, but figured their split of the Flamingo's "take," even after his skim, would quiet the wolves. He spent the morning of **June 20, 1947** in Los Angeles getting a haircut, and finally visiting "Jack's on the Beach" in Santa Monica for lunch. It was a good day for Siegel. The weekly sheets from the casino showed profits still increasing. His daughters, Barbara and Millicent, had been put on a train in New York City by their mother, Esta, to stay with him in Vegas for the summer. Siegel ran errands for the remainder of the afternoon, and finally returned with his pals, Allen Smiley and Chick Hill, in early evening to Virginia Hill's mansion on North Linden Drive in Beverly Hills.

Bugsy Siegel was shot to death on June 20, 1947. He was hit four times, once in the eye and three times in the chest.

Siegel carried a paper he'd picked up at Jack's On The Beach, and moved directly into the living room. Curiously, he caught the scent of flowers, carnations, but there were no flowers in the house. Chick Hill had gone to his room upstairs. '

Bugsy Siegel turned on a table lamp, and dropped on to the sofa. Allen Smiley trailed Siegel into the room and sat beside him. Siegel was about to begin reading his paper when shots range out.

Smiley hit the "deck" and was not hit. One shot took out Siegel's eye, and three more tore through his chest. The gunman was perched on a pergola in a rose garden just outside Siegel's window. It was obvious even at a distance that his contract had been fulfilled, and the gunman stole off into the night, disappearing without a trace. The newspaper Siegel had never read was stamped. "Good Night. Sleep Well. Compliments of Jack's On The Beach."

Chapter 12
The Kefauver Hearings

and Frank Costello

The Kefauver Hearings
and Frank Costello

With the "permanent" solution to the Bugsy Siegel problem taken care of, Meyer Lansky's people took over the Flamingo. That was just the beginning, as Lansky put together various combinations of syndicate members to franchise an entire "strip" of resort casinos in Las Vegas. Johnny Scalish and Moe Dalitz in Cleveland, Joe Lombardo and Ray Patriarca in Massachusetts and Rhode Island, and Stephano Magaddino pooled their resources to take "points" in the Thunderbird and Desert Inn in Vegas, and similar Lansky enterprises, first in Havana, and later the Grand Bahamas. The Sands, Dunes, Sahara, Riviera, Tropicana, and Caesar's Palace all had "silent partners" in their early years, directing their gambling activities.

Moe Dalitz, a long time Lansky associate, coordinated the casino "take" and the distribution of profits to the distinguished investors. In due time, Jimmy Hoffa would make the vast resources of the Teamsters Central States Pension Fund available to Lansky for further acquisitions.

The man to get a "loan" application into Hoffa was Chicago insurance broker Allen Dorfman, who just happened to be the son of Red Dorfman, a "shooter" with not a few notches on his gun in the Chicago and New York gang wars of the 1930s. Many of the loans were then disbursed through the Continental Connectors Corporation of Hoffa's attorney, Morrie Schenker.

Over 20 years, some $50,000,000 of Teamster money found its way into the mob's gambling business through Lansky's "lending" apparatus. But the mob's "dark prince" wasn't finished with his financing magic on the Vegas strip. It was Lansky who enticed Howard Hughes into "cleaning up" the strip by buying most of the major resort casinos. The Mob reaped enormous profits when the Hughes deals closed, and then bought in again, "cheap," when Hughes became disenchanted in the early 70's, finding to his chagrin that it wasn't quite as easy as he thought it would be to operate the gambling meccas above board, and "on the up and up."

The post-war years were literally a bonanza for the mob, nationally and in upstate New York. Most of the bosses remained anonymous. There were few headlines. With Lucky Luciano "retired" in Naples, his name soon disappeared from the print media, while his narcotics smuggling apparatus flourished.

Beginning in Turkey, thence to the south of France, Marseilles and the smack refineries, by sea to Montreal, then down the St. Lawrence into Lake Ontario to Toronto, Guelph and Hamilton, and into the States at Niagara Falls and Buffalo, and finally downstate to the New York hub for the tri-state area, or via Windsor and Detroit into the mid west, the "pipeline" brought in the Number Four White Injectable, generating profits of more than $150,000,000 each year.

Settimo "Big Sam" Accardi, the Volpes in Toronto, and Lou Greco in Montreal coordinated the smuggling operation for Don Stephano. Periodic meetings were hosted by Don Stephano at the Pinetree Stables in Framingham, Massachusetts, on the neutral turf of New England bosses Joe Lombardo and Ray Patriarca, to insure that the "pipeline" remained open and profitable. And for years it did.

Magaddino also shared in a lucrative trucking business put together by old pals Joe Zerilli and Tony D'Anna, in Detroit. Ford had major manufacturing facilities in Detroit, the Province of Ontario, Buffalo, and Edgewater, New Jersey. Automobiles had to find their way to major retail markets downstate in New York. Car transporters answered to the mob's businessmen bosses and Ford had no choice but to make appropriate deals to get their cars to market.

Magaddino had pioneered mob involvement in beer and liquor distribution, and he again took "points" in a deal structured by Frank Costello to combine various captive distributorships and distilleries. Longy Zwillman controlled the Brown-Vintners liquor importing firm, and he struck lucrative deals for his mob partners in a sale to Seagrams. He later repeated that "success" with Reinfeld Importers Ltd., the exclusive importer and distributor of Gordon's Gin, and Haig & Haig Scotch.

The "upstate" boss also took "points" in the mob-controlled gambling complex at Saratoga, just a stone's throw from the State House in Albany that then was still occupied by Tom Dewey.

There were lavish casinos and back room bust-out joints, all of them illegal, and operating with "protection" from resident authorities and highly placed persons in the State government. Arrowhead, the Chicago Club, Delmonico's, Piping Rock, Newman's Lake House, and Smith's Interlochen were all familiar wagering holes.

The period from **1946 to mid-1950** was perhaps the mob's "golden era", despite the necessity of Luciano "ruling" in absentia. The mob's ingenuity in making a dishonest buck knew no bounds. Law enforcement literally did not seem interested as long as the organization's crimes "seemed" bloodless. J. Edgar Hoover, himself with a weakness for wagering on the ponies, refused to take the mob seriously and directed his federal police rather to combat the "red menace."

But all of that would change when the junior Senator from Tennessee put together a "road show" of hearings spotlighting the mob's big shots, and their activities. Estes Kefauver attended the meetings for the American Conference of Mayors and the United States Attorneys Conference in early 1950. The Mayors issued a position paper that organized crime was draining the economy's life blood and disrupting normal commerce.

Senator Kefauver presides over a committee hearing, a.k.a. the Kefauver Hearings.

The United States Attorneys' dismissed the organization as nothing more than an occasional aberration in certain major metropolitan areas. With such divergent opinions, Kefauver became intrigued with the problems and he became determined to find the truth of the matter. He was also aware that the publicity of such a probe might well pave his way to the White House. Kefauver pushed a resolution through the Senate creating a Special Senate Committee to Investigate Organized Crime in Interstate Commerce, and by **May of 1950**, Kefauver's Committee was ready to commence hearings.

His fellow probers included Senators Herbert R. O'Connor of Maryland and Lester C. Hunt of Wyoming, both Democrats, and Alexander Wiley of Wisconsin and crusty old Charles Tobey of New Hampshire, Republicans. Even more important than his fellow senatorial probers, Kefauver assembled an excellent investigative staff that dug deeply into the mob's activities in the prior 20 years.

For the first time ever, Congressional hearings were televised, and millions of people saw mob figures who spent lifetimes in the shadows. The Hearings lasted 16 months, from **May 1, 1950** to **Sept. 1, 1951**. They were held in 14 major metropolitan areas including New York, Philadelphia, Chicago, Los Angeles, and Las Vegas. With few exceptions, most major mob bosses were called to appear and testify, and after some predictable hassles over "ducking" the service of subpoenas, each took their turn before the hot TV lights and even hotter questioning from the Committee and its staff.

There were few answers, with most witnesses stumbling through repeated declarations of their Fifth Amendment privilege against self-incrimination. But answers really weren't expected. Questions typically took the form of long narrative descriptions of a particular crime, concluding with, "Isn't that so, Mr. _."

For the first time the vicious inner workings of the fight game were exposed. Jake LaMotta testified to throwing a 1947 fight with Billy Fox, and then paying the local 'don' $20,000, as the price of 'earning' his 1949 title shot with Marcel Cerdan. The mob's dirty linen was hung out to dry before the eyes of the largest TV audience ever. Organized crime as an enormous social, political and economic problem was now front page, and forever more would be the "target" of coordinated law enforcement and congressional strike forces.

* *

Frank Costello testifying before the Kefauver Committee in 1951.

As the cameras ground on, Frank Costello, Joe Adonis, Longy Zwillman, Willie Moretti, Mickey Cohen, Albert Anastasia, Carlos Marcello, Phil Kastel, Meyer Lansky, and Tony Accardo took their turns before the Kefauver Committee.

A few of the mob's luminaries, however, did succeed in avoiding the public scrutiny of the Committee. Vito Genovese took an extended Caribbean "holiday" that lasted 16 months. Unaccountably, neither Tommy Lucchese nor Stephano Magaddino were called. Nor was Joe Bonanno. There were comic moments. Willie Moretti rambling on, and saying nothing, his tongue loosened by tertiary syphilis and Virginia Hill, the mob's glamor girl "pillow," finally screaming at unrelenting reporters, "I hope an atom bomb falls on all of you." But the damage was done, especially to the underworld's hitherto anonymous "prime minister," Frank Costello.

It was Costello who held the organization together, stateside, for the absent Lucky Luciano. His success as Luciano's surrogate depended in large part on his anonymity, and ability to glide from crisis to crisis, as the deciding vote and voice of compromise. Costello's days before Kefauver's cameras ended his effectiveness.

Garrulous and uncooperative, Costello projected the image of the nasal thug, rather than the businessman he repeatedly professed himself to be. At one point Costello stormed from the hearing room, not to return until the Committee agreed to take the cameras off his face. From that point on only Costello's nervously clenching hands were shown, perhaps more telling of his predicament than his sullen face had been.

Frank Costello nervously clenched his hands while he testified.

Vito Genovese took it all in from the sanctuary of his yacht in Cuban waters. Genovese had for years believed that he, not Costello, should be Luciano's successor. Genovese did the dirty work in the narcotics business that returned enormous profits to the mob. Costello never had gotten his hands dirty, never, that is, until Kefauver got finished with him.

Genovese shrewdly judged that Costello was ripe for picking, and that Luciano was simply too far away to turn the tide.

The drift of what was happening was not lost on Luciano. Couriers made increasingly frequent trips to his villa in Naples. Vito Genovese was poised to strike, and Charlie Lucky dearly wished that old pal Bugsy Siegel was still around to take Vito out. But Siegel was gone, and with him went the independent "enforcement" arm that Luciano had so ruthlessly used to make stick every double cross that had gotten him to the top.

Vito Genovese's grab for the top was carefully orchestrated. First he moved against old time Luciano pal, Willie Moretti. Moretti, his tongue loosened by terminal disease, had talked much before the Kefauver Committee, but had actually said very little of any significance. Moretti's erratic behavior gave Genovese his chance to argue for Moretti's "retirement." The Commission reluctantly agreed.

On Oct. 4, 1951, Willie Moretti was shot dead.

On **Oct. 4, 1951**, Willie Moretti was shot dead as he began his lunch at Joe's Elbow Room in Cliffside Park, New Jersey. Joe Adonis, another Luciano loyalist, found himself in another kind of jeopardy. His appearance before Kefauver's Committee triggered State and Federal probes into his activities that ranged from gambling law violations at his Duke's Restaurant in Cliffside, New Jersey, to contempt of Congress charges, IRS charges, and charges that he had lied about his place of birth, stating Brooklyn to several bodies when in fact he had been born in a small town outside of Naples.

The gambling charges resulted in Joe Adonis going to jail for two years. Eventually he capitulated to the Immigration Service, agreeing in 1956 to deportation to Italy in return for the government dropping all remaining charges against him.

With Moretti dead, and Adonis ineffective because of problems with the law, Frank Costello's rule, as Luciano's - man depended on his ability to control the then dominant faction of the Commission, the triumvirate of Stephano Magaddino, Joe

Bonanno, and Joe Profaci. With their backing and the threat of Albert Anastasia's violence to back their edicts, Costello was for a time able to stalemate the moves of Vito Genovese. But Costello's lock on mob power was tenuous, at best. Magaddino was a long time partner of Luciano's in the smuggling business, but it was Genovese, not the exiled Luciano, who called the shots on the dope trade.

Bonanno was Magaddino's first cousin, and in many ways, his protege. But a rift was developing between them. Bonanno, youthful, tall, handsome and articulate, was the antithesis of his senior cousin, the rustic, brutish in appearance Stephano Magaddino. Bonanno was intent upon pushing his son, Bill, into the number two slot in his "family." Magaddino thought the move premature, and believed Gaspar DeGregorio, a more senior "family" member, was entitled to the position.

The aspirations of Bonanno for his son, Bill, could be overlooked by Magaddino, since they did involve an internal Bonanno "family" matter. Bonanno, however, was not content to remain quiet, while the mob's power base shifted in the direction of narcotics trafficking. First, Bonanno began infiltration of certain backwater west coast mob operations, hoping to incorporate them into his family; and from their base, build his own west coast empire.

Slowly, Bonanno's tentacles reached into Arizona, San Diego, and Los Angeles. Bonanno's west coast incursions seemed at first remote, and unimportant to the New York bosses. Later, he would embark upon a far riskier adventure, moving directly on Montreal, the hub of the Magaddino smuggling pipeline. And Bonanno was busy even closer to Magaddino's home base.

Frank Valenti was characterized as a capo in Bonanno's Brooklyn mob. Valenti had ties to Rochester, the "backdoor" to Magaddino's territory, and Bonanno early on ticketed Valenti as the instrument for close in pressure on Magaddino.

Frank Valenti

Prior to becoming Rochester's Mob Boss, Frank Valenti worked with John Sebastian LaRocca and Antonio Ripepi in Pittsburg.

But Frank Valenti had other ideas. He shrewdly judged that no one could take Magaddino head on. The time was not right for a move into the Flower City. An assortment of local bosses answered to Magaddino in Rochester, and Valenti bided his time, working with John Sebastian LaRocca, and Antonio Ripepi, in Pittsburg.

In the early 1950s, Angelo Acquisto, Magaddino's "underboss" in Buffalo, was caught siphoning profits. Again, Bonanno saw the upheaval in Buffalo as an excuse for Valenti to make his presence felt in Rochester. But Valenti demurred, remaining in Pittsburg. Magaddino quickly put his house in order, banishing Acquisto, and installing Fred Randaccio as "underboss." A Bonanno-Magaddino confrontation was avoided, but the clock was ticking.

In New York City, Vito Genovese continued his undermining of Frank Costello's position as Lucky Luciano's stateside representative. This time Tommy "Three Finger Brown" Lucchese was enlisted to get rid of Costello. Frank Costello got wind of the plot and, rather than dealing directly with Lucchese, elected to convene a committee of the Commission to deal with Lucchese, and in the process, expose Vito Genovese as the real trouble maker. Costello arrived at the meeting, properly escorted by his "underboss," Vito Genovese.

Joe Bonanno, Stephano Magaddino, and Joe Profaci would decide Lucchese's fate. Costello quickly laid out his evidence against Lucchese. The Committee, speaking through Profaci, asked Lucchese to state his side of the controversy. Lucchese remained silent. One by one, the Committee members interviewed Lucchese in private. Neither Profaci nor Magaddino had any success in persuading Lucchese to open up. Lucchese, however, did confide in Joe Bonanno. Lucchese simply stated that he struck out at Costello because Costello was plotting to kill him. Bonanno was incredulous. What was the source of Lucchese's information? Lucchese replied, "Vito". That admission stalemated the Committee. Costello had counted on them summarily disposing of Lucchese. By identifying Costello's own "underboss," Vito Genovese, as the source of the mitigating evidence, Lucchese made it impossible for the Committee to deal with him. He was, after all, only acting in "self defense." a circumstance always exempt from retribution.

Chapter 13

Vito Genovese and
Albert The Executioner

Then Apalachin

Vito Genovese and Albert The Executioner, Then Apalachin

Vito Genovese's move for the top spot in the mob did not

Vito Genovese was Frank Costello's Underboss, but he was making moves to take over his Boss's job.

go unnoticed. Albert Anastasia decided to take matters into his own hands.

First, he solidified his position within his Brooklyn territory, "electing" himself boss by orchestrating the murders of long time bosses Philip and Vincent Mangano in April of 1951.

Then, Anastasia sought Costello's approval for a direct move against Genovese. Costello again involved Joe Bonanno and Stephano Magaddino, seeking their advice. Vito Genovese was aware of what was happening, and he began making moves to orchestrate the murder of Albert Anastasia.

Bonanno and Magaddino narrowly averted a "blood letting" by persuading Anastasia and Genovese to meet face to face, and bury the hatchet. To the surprise of most intimates, Anastasia and Genovese did just that, shaking hands at the conclusion of the meeting hosted by Joe Bonanno. The lid stayed on, but the kettle continued to boil.

Albert Anastasia sought Frank Costello's permission to take out Vito Genovese.

Moves in the power game were not always of the "diplomatic" or "violent" variety. Joseph Bonanno strove mightily to avert a major mob cataclysm. But he continued his efforts to move in on Stephano Magaddino's operations, and prestige, by sometimes subtle devices. The marriage of his son, Bill Bonanno, to Rosalie Profaci, had not been arranged, but it fit perfectly into Bonanno's plotting.

When the mob's "royalty" convened for the reception at the Hotel Astor in New York City on **Aug. 18, 1956**, Bonanno took advantage of the occasion to forge new alliances. Mob minions from across the country paid their respects. Now, through his son Bill, Joe Bonanno literally was "family" with fellow mob leader Joe Profaci, the father of the bride.

When and if the time was ripe for a move on Magaddino, Bonanno would be able to count on Profaci as an ally. Don Stephano surveyed the impressive turn out and with brow creased, his expression showing the hint of a frown, he lamented, "Look at this crowd. Who the hell's going to be able to talk to my cousin now? This will go to his head."

The mid-fifties held one legal battle after another for Frank Costello. A contempt of Congress conviction for being evasive with Kefauver's probers was followed by a conviction for income tax evasion. Publicly compromised, and in prison for the first time in his life, Frank Costello came to a decision on the eve of his 64th birthday. He wanted out of the mob.

Word was quickly circulated to the senior members of the Commission. Costello's request was not without precedent. Owney Madden had been permitted to leave the New York rackets for a relatively tranquil retirement in Hot Springs, Arkansas. By **November of 1956**, Tommy Lucchese, Albert Anastasia, Joe Profaci, Joe Bonanno, and Stephano Magaddino had signaled their approval of Costello's request. Meyer Lansky and Longy Zwillman consented.

Vito Genovese had doubts about Costello's motives, but he, too, grudgingly agreed when the affirmative proxies of Lucky Luciano and Joe Adonis arrived from Italy. The decision of the "mafia princes" was confirmed at a meeting held in late 1956 in Apalachin, New York, at the home of Joe Barbara, an Endicott soft drink distributor who also happened to be a capo in the organization of Stephano Magaddino. Frank Costello walked out of prison in **March of 1957**, and into "retirement" at his Sands Point, Long Island Estate.

On **May 2, 1957**, Frank Costello joined some friends for drinks˜ at the Waldorf s Peacock Alley. The Costello party then adjourned to the fashionable east side restaurant L'Aiglon for dinner. Costello excused himself around 11 p.m. to take an expected call from his lawyer, Edward Bennett Williams. Costello took a cab to his Manhattan apartment, in the Majestic, located at 115 Central Park West, and exited the cab to enter the foyer without noticing the black Cadillac sedan that had pulled up behind his cab. Costello headed for the twin banks of elevators. As he passed, a fat man stepped from behind one of the foyer pillars. Pistol in hand, he called, "This is for you, Frank," following the maxim that a "don" deserved to get it from the front.

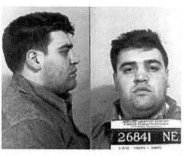

Above is a 1960 Mugshot of Vincent "The Chin" Gigante. Gigante did odd jobs for Vito Genovese including the May 2, 1957 botched "hit" on Frank Costello.

In that instant, Costello jerked his head to turn in the direction of the voice. The fat man snapped off a shot that would have been fatal had Costello not moved. As it was, Costello was grazed in the back of the head. Costello's assailant was the 300 pound, former middleweight fighter, Vincent "The Chin" Gigante, who did odd jobs for Vito Genovese.

Gigante, the fat man, disappeared when his pals deposited him upstate at a 'fat farm' where he lost 140 pounds and melted away into anonymity, until he resurfaced again in the eighties as underboss to Fat Tony Salerno, the then 'don' of the Genovese family.

Dazed and bleeding, Costello was taken to Roosevelt Hospital. Frank Costello survived and was released in a matter of hours. But his troubles continued to mount. While he received emergency treatment, Costello's clothes were searched. Police found a pencil written note stating "Gross Casino win — $651,284."

Investigation disclosed that the figure represented the exact "take" for the Tropicana Casino in Las Vegas for the prior 24 days. The Nevada Gaming⁻ Commission launched hearings and Costello faced a jail term, and again he petitioned the Commission for permission to retire. Vito Genovese admitted that he had ordered the hit on Costello because Frank had been meeting secretly with Albert Anastasia and plotting against him. Costello denied it, but this time he was permitted to go quietly into retirement.

With Costello neutralized, Albert Anastasia and Vito Geno-vese began the ritual dance of accusation and cross accusation that would only end when one of them killed the other. Genovese struck first, killing two of Anastasia's Lieutenants, the brothers Frank and Joe Scalise. With the Scalise brothers gone, Carlo Gambino became Albert Anastasia's number one lieutenant. Gambino counselled conciliation, and for a time Anastasia backed off while he made his case against Genovese with the other bosses so that they would back his play when it came. Anastasia hesitated also because he was temporarily about other business.

Meyer Lansky had put together a lucrative gaming operation in Cuba under the protection of Fulgencio Battista, the dictator again in power. Lansky's associates in Cuba included Moe Dalitz and Johnny Scalish from Cleveland, Russell Bufalino from Buffalo and northern Pennsylvania, and Santos Trafficante, the Florida boss. In the past, Lansky had put together syndicate combinations to share gambling profits, generously piecing off his partners while retaining just enough to insure continuing control of the venture.

Anastasia hadn't been asked (to be cut) in to Cuba by Lan-sky. Had he done so, Lansky might have accommodated him, even though there was a long standing animosity between the intellectu-al Lansky, and the man he considered a brutish killer. Anastasia elected to muscle his way in by turning Santos Trafficante against Lansky. This proved to be a fatal error.

Trafficante signaled Lansky. Lan-sky let it be known that he would back Vito Genovese if Vito moved against An-astasia. Genovese got to Anastasia's un-derboss, Carlo Gambino, and succeeded in persuading him to look the other way. Russell Bufalino huddled with Stephano Magaddino, who decided that "peace" with Genovese, and a continuing "piece" of Lansky's Cuban action outweighed any gains from tipping Anastasia.

Crazy Joe Gallo

Genovese gave the Anastasia contract to Joe Profaci, who enlisted Crazy Joe Gallo to do the job. On **Oct. 25, 1957**, Albert Anastasia entered the barber shop at the Park Sheraton Hotel on Manhattan's westside. Anastasia's bodyguard conveniently took a walk.

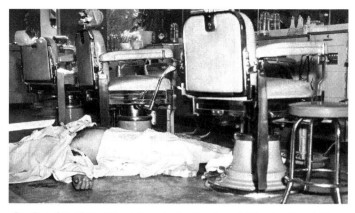

On Oct. 25, 1957 Albert Anastasia, the famed Murder Inc. killer, was murdered by Joey Gallo on the orders of Vito Genovese.

Albert Anastasia was settled in the barber chair, a hot towel over his face, when Joey Gallo and his back up entered the barber shop. Crazy Joe and friend pumped four slugs into Albert Anastasia, the last a finishing "head shot." Anastasia never saw it coming, and was dead before he hit the floor.

Albert Anastasia's death signaled a turmoil in the mob's hierarchy that continues to this very day. Crazy Joe Gallo believed himself entitled to greater "recognition" by boss Joe Profaci. To Profaci that meant a share of his take and territory. Joe Profaci refused, and for a time, Joe Gallo backed off, but the issue would flare again and again as Gallo's requests became increasingly insistent.

Vito Genovese renewed his efforts to be acknowledged by his partners in crime as boss of all bosses. The "retired" Frank Costello was powerless to stop him, with the removal of his "strong right arm," the brutal Albert Anastasia. The exiled Lucky Luciano watched and waited on developments from his Villa in Naples. So too did Joe Adonis in Milan.

The Chicago "outfit" was reorganizing, and for a time was non-committal. Paul "the waiter" Ricca, Tony "Joe Batters" Accardo, and Joey Aiuppa all dated back to Al Capone and Frank Nitti, and were the "shadow cabinet" in the "second city", but the man in the "lime light" was Sam Giancana. Sam Giancana had become the point man for the Chicago outfit and his lieutenants, Johnny Roselli and Johnny Formosa, were the men to see in Vegas and Hollywood.

Giancana had climbed to the top in the "Windy City", at least in part through the novel ploy of masterminding the kidnapping of his partners, and then earning their eternal gratitude by stage managing their safe return. Jake "Greasy Thumb" Guzik was one such victim. Eddie Jones, the black policy king of Chicago, was another. The Jones caper not only earned Giancana a piece of the policy action, but also $100,000 slice of the ransom.

**Sam Giancana,
Chicago Mafia Boss**

But there was more to Sam Giancana than just the ability to use the velvet glove to muscle in on the action. It was Giancana who began the mob's lucrative partnership with the Teamster's Union. Simply stated, the union loaned the money and the mob built the casinos.

Connections were cemented with Jimmy Hoffa, labor leader on the rise, and Allen Dorfman, Chicago insurance broker, who for decades would be the man to see in gaining an audience with the union power brokers. And there was more. Giancana instigated the naming of senior mob capos to key union positions, beginning with Johnny "Dio" Diogardi in Teamster Local 102 in New York City, and Anthony 'Tony Pro' Provenzano, in Teamsters Local 560 in Hoboken.

It was not always smooth sailing in the mob-union alliance. When syndicated columnist Victor Reisel exposed Johnny Dio's activities to take the union captive, Dio ordered an "object lesson" for the reporter. Acid was thrown in Reisel's eyes and he lost his sight. Dio's move was ill conceived. Reisel wasn't scared off. The headlines continued, but so, too, did the mob's infiltration of the unions.

Joe Bonanno continued his none too subtle moves that were designed to cut him a slice of the lucrative operations of other bosses. Bonanno still coveted Stephano Magaddino's strangle hold on the Montreal point of entry for the smuggling pipeline. But Magaddino seemed to be succeeding in heading off cousin Joe Bonanno by skillfully infiltrating contracting firms that had won rich government contracts for the completion of the enormous St. Lawrence Seaway construction project.

Undaunted, Bonanno turned his attention west, to backwater mob territories, a cheese operation in Wisconsin, a gambling venture in Kansas City, and finally, land speculating and construction businesses in Arizona. When Bonanno's agents began turning up in Las Vegas, Sam Giancana immediately put "two and two" together. Bonanno's Arizona presence was a smokescreen for a move on the Las Vegas rackets.

Vegas traditionally was an "open city" in mob parlance. Chicago ran it directly or through the captive Kansas City family for the benefit of all mob families holding "points" in Vegas casinos. Bonanno wanted to redefine the split. Giancana protested to Vito Genovese. Stephano Magaddino seized the opportunity to temporarily put a damper on cousin Joe Bonanno's activities on both coasts.

Magaddino contacted Vito Genovese and indicated that he would back Genovese's proposal for a "coronation" meeting if an emissary could personally contact Lucky Luciano in Italy and obtain his blessing for Genovese's elevation. Who better to see Charlie Lucky, suggested Magaddino, than his "trusted" cousin Joe Bonanno.

What Magaddino did not say was that Bonanno's absence from the country would give him an opportunity to extinguish the "brush fires" that Bonanno had started in Montreal. Genovese consented, and Bonanno was instructed to leave for Italy to seek Luciano's approval. Bonanno would take with him Carmine Galante, his strong arm capo, and John Bonventre, his uncle and consigliere. Sam Giancana, too, was placated. With Bonanno out of the country, Giancana and Johnny Roselli would have more than enough time to mend their fences in Vegas.

With Vito Genovese's meeting now a fait accompli, there remained only the fixing of the actual time and place of the meeting and the completion of preparations. Stephano Magaddino argued that Joe Barbara's home in Apalachin, the place of the 1956 meeting, should again be the site. A comfortable L-shaped two story stone faced home with striped awnings and spacious grounds, Barbara's home had indeed proven an out of the way location the year before in the sleepy hamlet of Apalachin.

The first mob meeting had gone unnoticed. Security had not been breached. But Sam Giancana had misgivings. In New York in July of 1957, to see the Floyd Patterson-Hurricane Jackson heavy-weight title fight, Giancana made a last ditch plea to move the meeting. Apalachin was too open. The parade of limousines with out of state plates could never go unnoticed a second time.

Giancana offered a number of locations in suburban Chicago as alternatives, reasoning that "captive" local police departments not only would never dare make waves, but would, to the contrary, actually insure security. Magaddino was not persuaded. His view prevailed, and the meeting was scheduled for Nov. 14, 1957.

Joseph Bonanno and John Bonventre returned from Italy on the eve of the Apalachin meeting. Stephano Magaddino was anxious to hear directly and in private from Joe Bonanno what Lucky Luciano had to say about the recent turn of events in New York. Bonanno and Magaddino would meet privately in Endicott on **Nov. 12, 1957**, before driving up to Joe Barbara's house.

Magaddino was accompanied by his brother, Nino, and John C. Montana, but neither stayed in Endicott with Stephano Magaddino. Both proceeded directly to Barbara's house. Stephano Magaddino and Joe Bonanno would catch up with them after their private talk.

Bonanno reported that Charlie Lucky was concerned that no further attempts be made on Frank Costello's life. With that as a quid pro quo, Luciano was willing to accept Vito Genovese' climbing to the top over Albert Anastasia's dead body, provided Genovese understood that his position as "chief executive" was, in matters of policy, still subordinate to 'Luciano's status as "chairman of the board." That pleased Magaddino who strongly opposed any retaliatory violence by Anastasia's "family."

Bonanno then launched into an "11th hour" plea to call off the meeting and reconvene it elsewhere in safer surroundings. Magaddino dismissed Bonanno's misgivings, saying simply that the meeting was Genovese's idea, and that, in any event, it was too late to do anything about it. Genovese was insistent that the Frank Costello situation and the assassination of Albert Anastasia be aired before all of the reigning mob bosses.

Genovese maintained that Anastasia's "sin" had not been plotting against him, but rather selling mob memberships for as much as $40,000 a head, contrary to the commission "freeze" on increasing the size of mob families. There were other matters, too, for discussion, including the Havana situation that was now in jeopardy with the insurgency of Fidel Castro, Joe "Socks" Lanza's problems in New York City at the Fulton Fish Market, and the mob's "piece" of the St. Lawrence Seaway and Niagara power projects, as well as military procurement in New York State.

Bonanno and Magaddino talked through the night of **Nov. 13**. On the morning of **Nov. 14**, the "cousins" adjourned their meeting to make for the mob convention at Joe Barbara's place. By that time, however, the State Police had already sealed off all roads to Joe Barbara's, and the mob round-up was on. Alerted, both Stephano Magaddino and Joe Bonanno avoided the dragnet and made their way home to Buffalo and New York City, respectively, by more circuitous, but "safer" routes.

* * *

Joe Barbara's 130 acre estate in New York's Southern Tier, above, was the site of the 1956 and 1957 Mafia Conventions.

The mob's Apalachin fiasco remains to this day a curious phenomenon. Certainly, Stephano Magaddino committed a terrible blunder in persuading his fellow bosses to assemble at Barbara's home. How the assembled "dons" thought they could go "unnoticed" in the rural locale remains a mystery to this day. Joe Barbara's 130 acre estate in New York's Southern Tier was located on McFall Road, a dirt road running between old Route 17, and Apalachin Creek.

Barbara, in the **Autumn of 1957**, owned the area Canada Dry distributorship, and fancied himself a rather low profiled "businessman," but his past had been checkered. Suspicions concerning the man ranged from bootlegging and gambling, to several gangland killings. On **Nov. 13, 1957**, Sergeant Edgar D. Croswell of the state Police was on routine patrol with a fellow trooper when he noticed "suspicious" out-of-state cars in the lot at the Parkway Motel in Vestal, a town just down the road from Apalachin. Suspicions aroused, Croswell alerted agents of the Alcohol and Tobacco Tax Division of the Federal Government, and the next day at 12:40 p.m., Croswell, partner Vincent R. Vasisko, and two ATT agents drove to Barbara's estate to make a routine check.

A typical mid autumn day, there were intermittent showers, fitful breezes, low scudding clouds, and temperatures in the 50's. Croswell's party had expected to find a few cars and to take plate numbers. They were shocked to find 10 cars in the parking area, and another 25 parked to the side near a barn. Croswell realized that they had stumbled on something entirely different than they had expected and his party withdrew to seek reinforcements. As they did, Mrs. Barbara happened to look out the window and sound the alarm, "There's the State Troopers!"

A road block was set up on old Route 17 near its junction with McFall Road. Other road blocks closed off alternative routes, and parties of agents closed off foot paths through the woods. Joe Barbara's guests panicked, and the Apalachin roundup was on. Nattily clad mobsters ran helter skelter through the woods, discarding bank rolls of pocket money in the thousands, wallets, "ID," and jewelry. One man, Simone Scozzari, produced a "roll" exceeding $10,000 and told Croswell he was "unemployed."

Two others said they were breaking in a new 1951 Chrysler and just happened to drop in on old pal Joe Barbara. Again, the mob was in the headlines. Vito Genovese, Carlo Gambino, Joe Profaci, Joe Magliocco, and some 60 others were identified as being at the meeting. Stephano Magaddino's insistence on the Apalachin location for the meeting had been, with-the benefit of "20-20" hindsight, a mistake of major proportions. A man of lesser stature surely would have paid with his life. As it was, Magaddino received "an earful" from Sam Giancana that is preserved in an FBI wire tap transcript, but nothing more.

Lost in the sensational headlines generated by Apalachin was the essential fact that no crime had been committed. True, the "dons" and their "capos" had assembled at Apalachin. But there was no testimony as to what transpired within Barbara's four walls. The essential underpinning for a conspiracy charge was missing. What was plotted, and by whom, remains to this day a mystery. Also, there was no RICO statute on the books in the late 50s. "Racketeering" was a prosecutorial catchword, but not then a federal crime, nor was "membership" in the mafia then deemed an indictable offense.

That would all change some 19 years later in New York City, but in 1957 the mob bosses were relatively safe from prosecution. The State Police cordon around Barbara's estate stampeded his guests into flight. It was a comical "catch-22" situation. They "ran" because they were being chased; they were "chased" because they ran. When the mobsters drove, walked, and ran helter-skelter from Barbara's home, they were detained and identified, and some were even arrested.

When, later, various investigatory bodies subpoenaed them to explain in sworn testimony why they'd assembled in Apalachin, their refusals to testify, or evasive answers, brought them contempt citations and jail time. But when appeals were finally perfected, nearly all of the contempt convictions were set aside.

Although Stephano Magaddino avoided capture, his underboss, John C. Montana, was not so fortunate. When State Troopers sealed off the area, John C. Montana attempted an escape on foot. Montana explained his "whereabouts" to an officer who detained him as "car trouble" while enroute to Pennsylvania. His cover blown, Montana returned to Buffalo to await the inevitable "weight" of public scrutiny.

With a business empire including two regulated businesses, liquor distributing from his Frontier Liquor Corp. in Buffalo, and Power City Distributing Co. Inc., a company jointly owned by the Magaddinos and Montana in Niagara Falls, and the major Buffalo taxi franchise operated by his Van Dyke Taxi and Transfer, Inc. as well as Montana Motors, Montana was well aware of his vulnerability. He "willingly" gave testimony to State and Federal grand juries and commissions probing Apalachin. It was almost enough to weather the storm, but not quite.

The little things piled up to trip Montana. He had arrived at Joe Barbara's home at 2:30 p.m. when the "car trouble" occurred. Yet troopers indicated that they had sealed the area with roadblocks around 1 p.m. Montana was simply leaving after calling for car repairs when troopers apprehended him. Why then was he found in the woods in disarray, running on foot, finally caught on barbed wire, and out of breath with shoes muddied?

A perjury prosecution wound down to acquittal. But then old friend Sam Lagattuta, an associate in Montana Motors, who in fact was John C. Montana's bodyguard, dodged probers until his arrest on **Dec. 12, 1958**, a circumstance that rekindled the "heat" on Montana. The State Liquor Authority came down on him, revoking bonds and license for his liquor distributorships.

A trial for conspiring to obstruct justice commenced in **November of 1959**, a charge that really translated to "keeping bad company" at Apalachin. An officer charged Montana with offering a bribe to suppress his testimony as to Montana's conduct at Apalachin, but later recanted the charge under cross-examination at trial.

John C. Montana

Montana may have hurt his cause by promising to take the stand in his defense, a stratagem he later reconsidered on the advice of counsel, but not before the press widely publicized his "willingness" to testify under oath and be cross-examined.

In November of 1959, John C. Montana was tried for conspiring to obstruct justice. He was found guilty and sentenced to four years in prison with a $10,000 fine. But he was spared prison time when that conviction was reversed the following year.

Some 50 prominent Buffalo business people testified to Montana's good character at the trial. It wasn't enough, though, as Buffalo's "man of the year" fell to the weight of prosecutorial perseverance, being sentenced to four years in prison with a $10,000 fine.

Many a resident of Buffalo in the fifties couldn't believe that the civic minded John C. Montana was indeed the Don's man in Buffalo. But the "signs" were there for anyone willing to look closely. Brother-in-law to Magaddino, when Montana's nephew married one of the Don's daughters, Frank Costello was the honored guest at the gala wedding bash held at the Statler Hilton. Nephew Russell Bufalino, Pennsylvania-Binghamton boss, also was in attendance.

Discredited, in many ways a broken man, Montana was spared jail time when the Second Circuit Federal court of Appeals reversed his conviction in November of 1960, holding that there was no evidence in the trial record to show violations of State or Federal law or any conspiracy to violate them. A heart attack killed Montana at age 70 on March 18, 1964.

Montana was not alone in coming a cropper the Apalachin dragnet. Frank Valenti and brother Constenze "Stanley" Valenti were jailed in **September 1958,** after refusing to answer questions by the New York State Commission of Investigation concerning the mob convention. Frank Valenti appeared on the first day of hearings, **Aug. 12, 1958**, before the State Investigation Commission (SIC).

Some 26 questions were propounded to Valenti, which he declined to answer by reason of potential self-incrimination. The SIC thereupon granted Frank Valenti "immunity" and repeated the questions. When Valenti again refused to answer he was remanded to a "show cause" hearing in State Supreme Court to determine whether he should be committed to civil jail until he agreed to answer questions.

Arguments that the SIC was incompetent to grant "immunity" and had in any event, watered down any such grant by agreeing to pass its information on to other bodies, were summarily rejected. Breaking new ground, the Court refused bail and committed Valenti to New York's civil jail on West 37th Street where presumably he would remain until he saw the error of his ways

Frank Valenti (left) and Stan Valenti (right) both attended the infamous Apalachin Summit in 1957 and both were jailed for refusing to answer questions about the meeting.

and decided to answer. Brother Stanley soon followed. The brothers Valenti finally agreed to give the SIC's questions another go, but said little other than that they had dropped in on Barbara to visit him after his "illness," and that they had no idea who the other assembled guests were or why they just happened to pick the same time to drop in.

The succession of chance visits to a "sick" friend simply failed to persuade the authorities. Why, they asked, had "sick" and "failing" Joseph Barbara placed an order with Armour and Company of Binghamton on Nov. 5, 1957 for 207 pounds of steak, 20 pounds of veal cutlets, and 15 pounds of luncheon meat. The Valenti's stuck with their story.

"No improvement," said the Court, and again the Valentis were jailed, this time to await the outcome of their appeals. When finally their cases reached the Court of Appeals in 1959, Frank was freed because a majority of the Court agreed that his answers were not patently evasive and unresponsive, nor were they so incredible as to be beyond belief. Brother Stanley was not so fortunate, remaining in jail for several additional months before he, too, was finally released.

Even Don Stephano Magaddino himself could not completely avoid the afterwash of the Apalachin fiasco. State Troopers, who found it impossible to serve a subpoena to take his testimony, hit upon the expedient of staking out a polling place in November of 1958 in the hope that the Don, a man fiercely proud of his American citizenship, would appear to vote. When his limousine arrived, Magaddino was duly served, despite his protest that he was only a salesman for the Camellia Linen Supply Co. Someone apparently feared what the Don might say and tossed a grenade through his window on **Nov. 10, 1958**, the night before he was to testify. Fortunately for Magaddino, the grenade was a dud. It was all for naught though as the Don took the Fifth 37 times at his hearing, adding nothing to the tale being woven by law enforcement agencies.

Chapter 14

The Downfall of Vito Genovese

The Coming of The Kennedys

And Cuba

The Downfall of Vito Genovese, The Coming of The Kennedys, And Cuba

Apalachin was not the only point of vulnerability for the mob in 1957. Senator John McClellan empaneled the Senate Select Committee on Improper Activities in the Labor or Management Field. The McClellan Committee numbered Senator John Fitzgerald Kennedy of Massachusetts among its members, and appointed his brother, Robert Kennedy, Chief Investigative Counsel.

Robert Kennedy's dedication to rooting out mob infiltrators in labor unions bordered on the messianic. Quickly he targeted Jimmy Hoffa as public enemy #1 in the unions. But more important even than the Kennedy-Hoffa vendetta, was Kennedy's success in finally compelling J. Edgar Hoover to unleash the full force of the FBI against organized crime.

J. Edgar Hoover

Hoover, for reasons never fully articulated on the public record, had not viewed the mob as a priority target for his federal police agency. When the bureau was in its infancy, the G-Men targeted the depression bank robbers, John Dillinger, Pretty Boy Floyd, Baby Face Nelson, and the rest. During Prohibition there were cooperative efforts with state and local law enforcement agencies against bootleggers.

Subversive activity occupied the Bureau during the war, and after came the McCarthy years and the crusade against communism. The capture of Lepke had been a notable exception to the Bureau's disinterest in the mob. There was also another more curious episode. Beginning in the 30's and continuing through the 40's, the FBI received the "gift wrapped" disclosures of Nicola Gentile, a disaffected "don" exiled to Sicily by the Commission.

The Bureau apparently "filed" Gentile's tales until Joe Valachi rolled over in the early 60's. In the late 50's, however, the headlines and results generated by the Senate's racket busting apparently finally persuaded the "Director" to move with dispatch against the mobsters.

Hoover had reservations about Robert Kennedy that had their genesis in the activities of Joseph Kennedy, the patrone of the Kennedy clan, decades before. Hoover was aware of the fact that Joe Kennedy had at least in part accumulated his vast fortune by an "unholy alliance" with Frank Costello in smuggling liquor during prohibition. But more than that, Joe Kennedy's extra curricular activities in his personal life troubled Hoover.

Joe Kennedy had carried on a notorious liaison with screen star Gloria Swanson in the 20's and 30's. So infatuated with Swanson was Kennedy that he personally financed her 1928 film, "Queen Kelly". Directed by Eric von Stroheim, "Queen Kelly" was an unmitigated $1,000,000 artistic and financial fiasco. Kennedy was forced to pull the plug on the production. But Gloria Swanson held on to the footage for some 20 plus years before it turned up on her personal viewing screen in scenes she played as Norma Desmond, the fading silent screen star in Billy Wilder's classic "Sunset Boulevard".

Joe Kennedy (above) was one of many people J. Edgar Hoover kept files on.

Hoover was an enigmatic, even paranoid person. His dossiers on the rich and powerful in the government establishment were notorious. But notwithstanding his characteristic "distrust," for Hoover there was a flaw in the Clan Kennedy that bore watching. They made a dollar where they could, even in concert with a gangster, and perhaps even more telling, they were indiscreet. The question was whether the sins of the father would be passed on to the sons.

"Apalachin", rather than the occasion for his coronation, became the beginning of "Armageddon" for Vito Genovese. Genovese's troubles began in an unanticipated quarter. From its beginnings, Genovese's relationship with his wife, Anna, was enigmatic, and, at times even murderous. Genovese became involved with Anna when she was married to another man. Genovese ordered the murder of his rival, who disappeared without a trace. During his lengthy absences from the country, Vito Genovese left his books to Anna for safe keeping and updating. Anna faithfully recorded the details of Vito's illicit transactions and increasingly gave in to her proclivities for promiscuous liaisons.

Vito Genovese had left Anna "in the care" of Steve Franse during his extended stay in Italy during and after World War II. Franse apparently became "involved" with Anna. Genovese was thousands of miles away, but Anna's transgressions could not have gone unnoticed. When Genovese returned in the late 40s, a domestic explosion was expected. It didn't happen. By the time "Apalachin" took place, Genovese had climbed to the top of the mob. Apalachin again made Vito Genovese and his fellow mob bosses "public" at a time when they could ill afford the publicity. With "Apalachin" an accomplished fact, mob bosses laid low in its aftermath to cut their losses.

Genovese was occupied with ducking an army of process servers intent upon subpoenaing him for appearances before federal, state, and local law enforcement agencies. It was at this moment of his maximum vulnerability that Anna Genovese turned publicly on her husband. A beating at Genovese's hand sent Anna into the offices of the FBI in Manhattan. She detailed Vito's womanizing and his marital brutality.

Anna and Vito Genovese.

More importantly, she showed the FBI "page and verse" on Genovese's dirty money. Not the "penny ante" grifter of his "tongue in cheek" public posturing, Vito Genovese was shown to be the kingpin of an enormous personal fortune. Profits rolled in weekly in cash increments of $40,000. Genovese's fortune was estimated to be more than $30,000,000. IRS commenced an investigation that Genovese knew could eventually take him down.

The New York City criminal fraternity waited on Genovese to take his vengeance on Anna. Anna Genovese had refused protective custody. Curiously, Genovese did not move against her. Rather, he sent her a non too subtle message, the "garrote" murder of her lover, Steve Franse, in a restaurant owned by Joe Valachi. While the IRS probe of Genovese geared up, the FBI received another "gift horse" that would make far quicker work of Vito Genovese than the tax man.

In mid 1958 a low level narcotic pusher, Nelson Cantellops, was arrested by the FBI. Cantellops told of witnessing "deals" involving Genovese's senior lieutenants, and finally a meeting that included Genovese where Vito himself ordered his boys to move in and take over narcotics distribution in the East Bronx. It was too good to be true. A junior "punk" like Cantellops didn't figure to have such information. But after hundreds of hours of interrogation, Cantellops held up.

Genovese was charged with conspiracy to distribute narcotics. The case reached trial in April of 1959. Nelson Cantellops delivered a bravura performance on the stand. Genovese's lawyers could not shake him. The verdict was "guilty," and Genovese was sentenced to 15 years in the federal penitentiary. To this day, persons in law enforcement believe that Cantellops was "programmed" to take Genovese down, and a rumor persists that Cantellops tongue was loosened by a $100,000 "donation" from fellow mob bosses who believed Vito Genovese's time had come.

Fulgencio Battista had long been a "friend" of the mob in Cuba. As suitcases of cash were deposited into his numbered Swiss accounts, the mob's Cuban Casinos flourished. But "revolution" flashed against Battista in the mid 50's and the tide turned for the guerrilla fighters of Fidel Castro in Cuba in Mid-1957. Meyer Lansky read the trend correctly, and began moving mob money to the casino and resort industry in the Grand Bahamas.

Havana, like Las Vegas, was considered an "open city" for the mob. Any mob family with the money and the inclination was entitled to take points in the Havana casinos, racetracks, and brothels. The managers were Lansky's men, who answered to him as "trustees" for the entire organization.

First among them was Santos Trafficante, the Florida boss, who split time between Miami and Havana. One senior lieutenant was Russell Bufalino, Stephano Magaddino's man in the Caribbean. Racetracks were Bufalino's specialty. Johnny Roselli, the mob's point man in Vegas, also worked the San Souci casino in Havana, as well as the Deauville and Commodoro. Roselli had, with the passing of Bugsy Siegel, become the mob's man in Hollywood.

John Roselli, above, worked for Chicago Mafia Boss, Sam Giancana.

It was Roselli who engineered the shakedowns of Joseph Schenck, one of the founders of Twentieth Century Fox, through mob shills Willie Bioff and George Browne, which eventually landed Schenck in jail. And Roselli backed the notorious Harry Cohn when Cohn needed funds to complete his takeover of Columbia Pictures. Roselli was also "eyes and ears" for Sam Giancana, the Commission member responsible for co-ordinating all of the mob's activities in gambling and entertainment.

Sam Giancana traveled to Havana in **June of 1958** to assess the mob's options in Cuba. He met there with Santos Trafficante, Johnny Roselli, and Russell Bufalino. Trafficante counseled conciliation with Castro, figuring that Castro, like Battista, could be bought, and misjudging completely Castro's revolutionary fervor. For Sam Giancana, the problem was elementary. Castro had to go, and the sooner the better.

John Roselli added that he had run into government types in the San Souci, who had expressed an interest in dealing with the mob to get close to Castro. While the mobsters were meeting, the radio blared out news of Raul Castro, Fidel's firebrand younger brother, kidnapping 27 U.S. sailors and marines outside the naval base at Guantanamo. Giancana exploded, "That's it! The bum's got to go." Still, Trafficante wasn't persuaded. The meeting concluded with no clear consensus.

Trafficante would work to get close to Castro to do some business. Giancana instructed Roselli to find the government men again, and determine just what exactly they had in mind. Within days, Raul Castro released the U.S. servicemen. And for a time, it was business as usual for the mob in Havana.

Russell Bufalino returned to New York to report on the Havana situation to the New York bosses and Stephano Magaddino. Unfortunately for Bufalino, the shores of the United States proved equally as hostile as the climate in Havana. Bufalino was arrested in New York and branded an undesirable alien. A deportation hearing was scheduled in September of 1958. Immigration authorities hammered away at technical violations of regulations governing aliens. Bufalino had failed to register and report his address. He had lengthy absences from the country, most often in the Caribbean.

Russell J. Bufalino, right, and Thomas Lucchese testify before the Senate Rackets Committee, in Washington, on July 3, 1958.

More importantly, the Immigration Service contended that Bufalino had made false statements upon entering the country, specifically in failing to disclose his itinerary in Cuba, Bimini and the Bahamas when he re-entered the country in 1956. Round one was lost by Bufalino, but the deportation order was stayed on **Sept. 12, 1958**, pending appeal.

By the end of 1958, the mob's fortunes clearly were in eclipse in Havana. Castro's triumphant columns were coming out of his mountain redoubts for the final march on Havana. Sam Giancana signaled mob managers to salvage what they could and leave the city. Only Santos Trafficante, among the senior mob operators, elected to remain. Trafficante still believed he could strike a deal with Castro.

On **Nov. 23, 1958**, Ambassador Earl E. T. Smith reported to President Eisenhower that the Castro movement was riddled with Communists. Ken Redmond, the President of United Fruit Company, released a statement to the press on **Dec. 3, 1958** that Castro was a clear threat to the orderly and profitable marketing of the huge Cuban sugar crop.

On **Jan. 1, 1959**, Fidel Castro entered Havana and rang down the curtain on the Battista era. Santos Trafficante finally arranged a face to face meeting with the new Cuban strongman. Trafficante left the meeting with an air of optimism. Within a month, however, Trafficante was languishing in a Cuban prison at Trescornia.

Through the **late summer of 1959**, Castro flashed inconsistent signals, both to the U.S. government and to the owners of Havana's lucrative casino and resort industry. Sam Giancana saw Castro as nothing but an enemy. The CIA, even at that late date, wasn't so sure.

In **November of 1959**, General Charles Cabell, the deputy director of the CIA, reported to the Senate that, in his judgment, Fidel Castro was not a communist, and that he doubted that the eastern bloc was interested in recruiting him.

Santos Trafficante

Castro permitted Santos Trafficante visitors. Jack Ruby, a mid-level Chicago Gangster turned strip club impresario living in Dallas, was admitted to the country to see Trafficante. Ruby played middle man as a deal was struck between Castro and the Mob to free Trafficante. By the end of 1959, Santos Trafficante was again in the United States. But before Trafficante and Meyer Lansky could act to implement a new arrangement with Castro, the Mob participated in an incident that sealed forever their fate with the Cuban dictator.

An underground cell of Cuban exiles operating in Havana used **January of 1960** to shop for explosives to create an incident that would begin the undermining of Castro's authority. Mob members in hiding in Havana were all too eager to oblige the dissidents, and a deal was struck pursuant to which the mob provided a cache of explosives.

In **March of 1960**, a French freighter loaded with 76 tons of Belgian rifles and grenades anchored at Mariel harbor. Within days of its arrival, a tremendous explosion demolished the freighter. Hundreds of dock workers were killed and injured. Castro needed no road map to point the finger of responsibility.

President Eisenhower responded to Castro's verbal barbs by threatening to cut the import quota for the Cuban sugar crop, which represented 80 percent of Cuba's exports, and 30 percent of its national income. Castro, not to be outdone by the American President, went public with his plan to purchase whole factories for heavy industry from eastern block countries, and crude oil from Russia. The appropriation of U.S. lands in Cuba began, and Castro demanded that the great Texaco, Shell, and Standard oil refineries process the Russian crude.

In late **March of 1960**, the CIA sold President Eisenhower on its plan-to train Cuban exiles in Guatemala for an eventual invasion of Cuba. Comprehensive anti-Castro broadcasts began from a CIA radio beacon on Great Swan Island, 400 miles due south of Cuba.

By **June of 1960**, Fidel Castro was regularly exchanging verbal brickbats with American government officials in the international press. The clock clearly was ticking on a final confrontation between the Yankees and the Cuban strongman, and the mob was loving every minute of it.

Maybe the Havana goldmine wasn't lost, after all. Sam Giancana was sure he would finally get his shot at Castro. He wasn't far wrong. Johnny Roselli reported to him the CIA agents had surfaced with a proposal that the mob "hit" Castro and in return again receive the Havana gaming concession under a friendlier successor regime. The deal was struck and the mob began planning Castro's demise.

The Gangster Chronicles is a four part series that documents Italian organized crime from its inception until modern day times. The series is presented in four parts primarily due to the extensive amount of information presented.

The Gangster Chronicles Part Two is Coming Soon!

Part Two will feature:

Castro

The Kennedy's

Marylyn Monroe

Oswald

Ruby

Hoffa

Joe Columbo

Crazy Joe Gallo

And much more!

Endnotes for Chapters 1-14

Sources are cited in full at first reference, then abbreviated as indicated thereafter. References are to statements identified by quoted first three words. Note: Where used herein, the term "faction" means a type of historical word rooted in fact.

Chapter 1:The Beginning: Mussolini Comes To Power (pgs. 7-12)

"their turn marched": Alfonso Lowe, Sicily, the Barrier and the Bridge, Norton, 1972, 12-14,and bibliography, 193-95 (hereinafter "Lowe"), and Nicholas Gage, Mafia, U.S.A., Playboy Press Books, 1972, at 59-79 (hereinafter "Gage")

"All of it a breath away": Gay Talese, Maida in Esquire, September, 1986, and Humbert S. Nelli, The Business of Crime, Oxford University Press 1976, at 3-23 (hereinafter "Nelli")

"fell upon his rear .guard": M.I. Finley, Denis Mack Smith, Christopher Duggan, A History of Sicily Viking 1987, bibliography 234-38 (hereinafter "Finley")

"'omerta', the code of silence": David Leon Chandler, Brothers In Blood, E.P. Dutton 8 Co. Inc. '1975, at 13 (hereinafter "Chandler")

"On October 30, 1922: Jerre Mangione, Mussolini's March On Rome, Franklin Watts, Inc. 1975.

"Mussolini received full": Benito Mussolini, Mussolini as Revealed in his Political Speeches 1914-1923, Howard Fertig 1976, in particular 171, 277.

"fugitives from justice": Denis Mack Smith, Mussolini, Alfred A. Knopf, Inc. 1982, at 93.

"evidence at trial": Chandler, at 54-55

"On that day in 1282": Joseph Bonanno, A Man of Honor, Simon and Schuster 1983 at 39 (hereinafter "Bonanno"), . Hank Messick and Burt Goldblatt, The Mobs and the Mafia, Galahad Books 1972, at 8-10 (hereinafter "Messick and Goldblatt"), and David Hanna, The Mafia: Two Hundred Years of Terror, Manor Books, Inc. 1979, at 10-11 (hereinafter "Hanna")

"voyage to America": Chandler, at 57, and Carl Sifakis, The Mafia Encyclopedia, Facts On File Publications, Inc. 1987, at 328 (hereinafter "Sifakis")

Chapter 2: The Mafia Migration/The Castellammarese Wars (pgs. 13-21)

"Cesare Mori had": Chandler, at 53-55, Sifakis, at 227.

"invented the pizzu": Chandler, at 56.

"Buffalo, or Detroit": Chandler, at 57, 135.

"the Buccillato Brothers": Bonanno, at 26.

"'godfather' to Don Ciccio's": Chandler at 54.

"'let no one dare'": Chandler at 54.

"The final leg": Bonanno, at 55-56.

"Neither man was hit": Bonanno at 63.

"First a mobster named Mimi": Bonanno at 78-80

"A homebody who": much of the Magaddino material is based upon the author's original research in the files of the Buffalo Evening News, and Courier Express, and Niagara Falls Gazette, and his personal interviews with Joseph "Spike" Lanovara, now in the Federal Witness Protection Program (hereinafter "Lanovara"), and the late William Mahoney, former Chief of Sheriff's Detectives for Monroe County (hereinafter "Mahoney").

"In Atlantic City": Sifakis, at 20.

"Prohibition was a bonanza": Sifakis, at 211.

"John C. Montana": Sifakis, at 262-63

"the Castellammarese pot": Richard Hammer, Playboy's Illustrated History of Organized Crime, The Playboy Press 1975, at 97, et seq. (hereinafter "Hammer")

"Maranzano's war 'treasury'": Bonanno, at 104 thru 122.

"St. Valentine's Day Massacre": Hammer, at 59-61.

Chapter 3:Luciano's Luck, Maranzano's Misfortune (pgs. 22-31)

"Milazzo, killing him": Bonanno, at 93.

"Aiello was murdered": Bonanno, at 120.

"had become Masseria's underboss": Tony Sciacca, Luciano, Pinnacle Books 1975, at 40 (hereinafter "Sciacca")

"Magaddino met with Luciano": Aloi, The Don No One Knew, unpublished manuscript (hereinafter "Aloi")

"another 'meet' with Charlie": Sciacca, at 87-88.

"the two men played cards": Hammer, at 111-112.

"Al Capone in Chicago": Sciacca, at 95-96.

"the arrangements were made": Bonanno, at 127-129.

"Vincent 'Mad Dog' Coll": Sciacca, at 102.

"'hard contract' to Bugsy Siegel": Sciacca at 103-105.

"stabbed and shot four times": Messick and Goldblatt, at 110-111.

"'the night of the Sicilian vespers'": Sifakis, at 240.

"as a national commission": Bonanno, at 141.

"infamous 'Murder Inc.'": Burton B. Turkus and Sid Feder, Murder, Inc., Bantam Books, 1951 (hereinafter "Turkus")

Chapter 4: The Cops, The Crooks, and the Big Rich, Chicago, After Capone. (pgs. 32-39)

"Al Capone had begun serving": John Kobler, Capone Fawcett Crest Books, 1071, at 306-307, 312-313 (hereinafter "Kobler")

"'the real' Jake Lingle": Jay Robert Nash, Bloodletters and Bad Men, Book 2, Warner Books 1975, at 78 (hereinafter Nash #2)

"concerning the life and times of Samuel Insull, see Marc Davis Rice and the Fall of Samuel Insull, Chicago Tribune 1994"

"'10 % Tony'": George Murray, The Legacy of Al Capone G.P. Putnam's Sons, 1975, at 169 (hereinafter "Murray")

"John Coughlin's First Ward Bill": Nicholas Von Hoffman, Organized Crimes Ballantine Books 1985. Von Hoffman reconstructs a First Ward bacchanal at pages 65-68.

"Samuel Insull": Geoffrey Perrett, America In The Twenties Simon and Schuster, Inc. 1982, at 343, 381, and 442 (hereinafter "Perrett")

"General Charles Gates Dawes": Perrett, at 131.

"Insull borrowed $48,000,000.": Perrett, at 442.

"another substantial Insull investor": original research by author in files of Chicago Tribune.

"Through Sam Ettelson": original research by author in archives of

Chicago Tribune, and Indianapolis Star.

"who had bet on Insull and lost": original research by author.

Chapter 5:   10 % Tony (pgs. 40-50)

"Roger Touhy, a bootlegger": John Morgan, Prince of Crime Stein and Day 1985, at 92 (hereinafter "Morgan")

"Frank Nitti said 'no dice'": Carl Sifakis, The Encyclopedia of American Crime 1982, at 718 (hereinafter "Sifakis/Crime")

"'the trump' on both": Ovid Demaris, Captive City Lyle Stuart, 1969, and Jay Robert Nash, People To See, An Anecdotal History of Chicago's Makers and Breakers, New Century Publishers, Inc. 1981, bibliography at 247-255.

"Nitti was bundled": Murray, at 175-76.

"Dillinger began his sentence": Nash #2, at 139.

"Anton Cermak had won": Murray 176-177.

"Frank's plan to have a piece of the action": Nitti's, "alliance" with the depression era bank robbers was in the author's view based on their ability to provide the Chicago "outfit" with the weapons it needed to police captive rackets, and also the plain fact that they hogged the press and kept the "outfit" out of print. The inventories of several of the armory robberies pulled by Dillinger and company indicate that the number of weapons stolen were so great that they could only have been fenced through the "outfit".

"Gunner Jack McGurn knew": Original research by author in files of Chicago Tribune and Chicago Sun-Times; Jay Robert Nash, The Dillinger Dossier 1983 (hereinafter "Nash/Dillinger"). The reconstruction of the incident at Wrigley Field is "anecdotal" based on the information available.

"at Wrigley Field between the Bears": the author's reconstruction of the incident at Wrigley Field is anecdotal based upon the information available.

"Campagna boarded the train": "Little New York's" presence in Miami is likely based on available evidence. Nicholas Von Hoffman and Max Allan Collins reconstruct this event in their "faction" novels, Organized Crimes, and True Crime, respectively.

"Joseph Zangara was convicted": Sifakis, at 350-51; Nash #2, at 425-27.

"Jake 'the Barber' Factor": Murray, at 148.

"Tuohy severed an artery": Murray at 149; as he lay dying,

Tuohy himself observed that the Chicago "outfit" had long memories indeed; unfortunately for Tuohy, he might have prompted those memories by publishing his autobiography, The Stolen Years, Pennington, 1959, on his release from prison.

Chapter 6:The Mob and Johnny Dillinger, The making of a Legend (pgs. 51-70)

"Dillinger and another man": Nash #2, at 137.

"Pierpont literally taught"- Nash #2 at 139-140.

"joined in a petition": John Toland, Dillinger Days, Random House. 1963, at (hereinafter "Toland"). Generally cited hereinafter for much of Dillinger material.

"As Dillinger Made Headlines": Toland, id.

"Matt Leach . . . Captain John Stege": Toland, id.

"Piquett became a 'counsellor'": Blackie Audett, Rap Sheet 1054, and Jay Robert Nash interviews with Audett.

"Louis Piquett who came up": Piquett's role in catalyzing the "alliance" between Nitti and Dillinger is deduced from his close relationship with both men, his admitted involvement with "outfit" fences, in particular, Jimmie Probasco, the mob's money launderer and resident plastic surgeon, and his well known penchant for finding colorful (if not overtly illegal) ways to turn a dollar. Probasco, like Piquett, may in a sense be the other "rosetta stone" to unlock the Dillinger switch mystery. Probasco would have been involved with both Dillinger and Jimmie Lawrence as plastic surgeon. He also was an intimate of both Nitti and Dillinger as a money fence. Plainly and simply, Probasco was in a position to know exactly what happened with Dillinger and Jimmie Lawrence. Probasco's mysterious end in a "brodie" from an office window in a Loop building that could have been part of an FBI suite may be proof that he indeed knew too much. It is believed in some quarters that the "feds" might have smelled the Jimmie Lawrence/John Dillinger switch and dangled Probasco by his heels over the Loop to improve his memory. The agents may have accidentally lost their grip, or dropped Probasco when he failed to sing.
"Their meeting was set": The Dillinger/Nitti alliance is subscribed to by Max Allan Collins as the basis for his "faction" novel, "True Crime" Tor 1984, bibliographical note at 372 and following. The genesis of the Dillinger/Nitti alliance and the Dillinger/ switch theory is the research of Jay Robert Nash and the disclosures of Jackie Audett, which are the subject matter of the previously cited Dillinger Dossier. Author Carl Sifakis questions that theory in The Encyclopedia of American Crime 1982, at 211.

"The men eyed each other": The Nitti/Dillinger meeting at the World's Fair is an anecdotal reconstruction by the author based on available information.

"'Kansas City Massacre": Richard Gid Powers, G-Men Southern Illinois University Press 1983 at 42-43 (hereinafter "Powers/G-Men")

"Bioff could never": Sifakis, at 35.

"Nitti spelled out his deal": The Nitti/Piquett meeting concerning Jimmy Lawrence is an anecdotal reconstruction by the author based on available information.

"Jimmy Lawrence looks": Nash #2, at 164-167.

"Sheriff Jess Sarbor": Nash #2, at 147.

"Something you don't"

"that your money": Nash #2, at 151.

"'Bucket of Blood' speakeasy": meeting between Nitti and Dillinger reconstructed by author based on materials in Nash, Dillinger Dossier statements of Blackie Audett, and reporters' recollections of statements by Louis Piquett.

"Mrs. Patzke replied": Nash #2, at 154

Chapter 7: Crown Point Then Little Bohemia (pgs. 68-86)

"Reaching El Paso": Dillinger's sojourn in the southwest is documented in the Nash, Dillinger Dossier , and novelized in Harry Patterson, Dillinger, Stein and Day 1983. The author's account is an anecdotal reconstruction based on available information.

"The sojourn in Tucson": Nash #2, at 154-56.

"I shot him"

"gang was returned to": Sifakis/Crime, at 208.

"none other than":   Blackie Audett disclosures.

"smiled knowingly, saying": the conversation between Dillinger and his lawyer is an anecdotal reconstruction based on available information.

"Piquett quipped to"

"Sergeant Martin Zarkovich": Sifakis/Crime, at 203-209. Sifakis believes that Louis Piquett bribed a Judge to get the gun to Dillinger. Piquett probably was the middle man, but Zarkovich seems more logical as the person who slipped Dillinger the real weapon. The author's deduction is supported by the plain fact that Zarkovich did indeed question Dillinger about the First National Bank of East Chicago, Indiana bank job, and thus had the opportunity to do what the "outfit" had ordered him to do, namely, help Dillinger to escape.

"a small plane"

"'I'd give you guys more'": Nash #2, at 156.

"as a movie producer": Nash #2, at 157.

"'there's a lot of heat'": the Nitti/Dillinger meeting on Malden is an anecdotal reconstruction by the author based on available information.

"Van Meter raked the door": Nash #2, at 158.

"'get to work and notify'"- Nash #2, at 158.

"Patton let the gang": Nash #2, at 159.

"so menaced Dr. Mortenson": Nash #2, at 160.

"agents R.L. Nalls": Nash #2, at 161.

"the story was leaked"

"the note stated that": the Nitti/Dillinger exchange at Wrigley Field is an anecdotal reconstruction by the author based on available information.

"'Oh, yes John'"

"'While I still have got'": J.E. Treherne, The Strange History of Bonnie and Clyde. Stein and Day, 1984, at (hereinafter "Treherne")

"'giving decent bank robbers'"

"Van Meter walked in": the conversation between Van Meter and Dillinger that night at Little Bohemia is an anecdotal reconstruction based upon available information.

"In Rhinelander": Powers/G-Men, at 120.

"Shoot to Kill": Powers/G-Men, at 121.

"Alerted by the gunfire": Toland, id.

"'Hull said a few words"

"'Republicans coming out'"

"greatly expanded 'powers': Powers/G-Men, at 121.

"In the next two months": Powers/G-Men, at 121- 122.

"Only the end of Bonnie": Treherne, at

"'Game Ends Where?'"   Power.-/G-Men, at 122.

"A petition for amnesty"   Toland, id.

"he 'liked Dillinger fine'"   Toland, id.

"The public outcry grew": This Fabulous Century 1930-1940
Time--Life Books, at 100-102.

Chapter 8: The Biograph, The Aftermath: Myth or Mystery
(pgs. 87-104)

"detectives Wright and Larsen": The murder of the East Chicago detectives is fact; the activities in the Bucket of Blood and Jimmy Lawrence'
participation in them are anecdotal reconstructions by the author.

"Zarkovich moved swiftly": The involvement of Sergeant Zarkovich in
the killings is deduced from his pivotal relationship to both Nitti, Dillinger,
and the federal police he ultimately used to bring to fruition Nitti's scheme to
dispatch a double in Dillinger's stead.

"The Service threatened Anna": Louis Piquett did represent
Anna Sage and was involved in defending her in the government's
deportation case. The meeting in Piquett's office attended by
Sage, Polly Hamilton and Bioff is an anecdotal reconstruction by
the author, based upon available evidence. There is a photograph
of Jimmy Lawrence with Polly Hamilton that seems to substanti-
ate their relationship.

"Zarkovich told Stege": Nash #2, at 163.

"Cowley, like John Stege": Toland, id.

"Anna Sage entered the Chicago office": Richard Gid Powers, Secrecy
and Power, The Life of J. Edgar Hoover, The Free Press/MacMillan 1987, at
191 (hereinafter "Powers/Hoover")

"French Napier, a Loop bookie": The existence of the bookie joint
above the Biograph seems rooted in the lore of the Loop. French Napier is
the anecdotal invention of the author.

"Martin Zarkovich coolly": Nash #2, at 164-65.

"Eyewitness accounts 'strangely'": Toland, id.

"is it - true?'"

"J. Edgar Hoover said": Powers/G-Men, at 125-129, and 137.

"For years, Hoover would say": Powers/G-Men, at 129.

"Audrey took one look":

"Death photos in the morgue": The circumstances of the post-shooting investigation and the forensics work-up, principally the autopsy, are exhaustively reviewed and analyzed in Nash' The Dillinger Dossier. The archives of the Indianapolis Star contain a number of interesting reminiscences from the "Dillinger Days". Of particular note is the series run by the Star which contained assertions by Dillinger's barber that not only was the man viewed at the Harvey Funeral Home not John Dillinger, but also, that Dillinger was seen in and about Mooresville on several occasions after his alleged shooting.

"The Associated press complained"

"It was the week before": the final meeting between Nitti and Dillinger behind the Kostur Hotel is an anecdotal reconstruction by the author.

"'Today I am the only man who knows'": Nash #2, at 167.

"Governor McNutt coldly turned down"

"Matt Leach, the tenacious": Toland, id.

"Polly Hamilton worked": Toland, id.

"Anna Sage was deported": Toland, id.

"Melvin Purvis expected to": Powers/Hoover, at 223-227.

"Willie Bioff was sent": Otto Friedrich, City of Nets, A Portrait of Hollywood in the 1940's Harper and Row, 1986, at 61-67 (hereinafter "Friedrich")

"Governor McNutt eventually pardoned": Toland, id.

"In his old age, Hoover"

"The Mex remained south": the events in Los Angeles after World War II involving John Dillinger are the invention of the author based on his deductions from available evidence.

"Jake Rubinstein whom, the Mex": Jack Ruby's involvement with Al Capone, then Frank Nitti as west coast liaison for the Chicago "outfit" was disclosed as early as the Kefauver Hearings in 1950. Whether Ruby ever crossed Dillinger's path in post war Los Angeles is purely the author's conjecture.

Chapter 9: New Directions After Prohibition (pgs. 105-111)

"These were tranquil days for Magaddino's": FBI/Organized Crime Taskforce/Alcohol, Tobacco, and Firearms briefing paper, 1977: FBI/Buffalo P.D. briefing paper and chart in files of Courier Express and Evening News: these materials were basic sources for the unpublished Aloi manuscript, The Don No One Knew, which deals extensively with the Buffalo crime family of Stephano Magaddino. (hereinafter "Aloi/Don")

"It was the Spring of 1932": reminiscences of Joseph "Spike" Lanovara, in particular, concerning Frank Camarrata and "the old days" in Cleveland.

"Charlie Lucky asked Magaddino": this exchange is an anecdotal reconstruction by the author; however, according to Lanovara and Camarrata, Magaddino and Luciano were well acquainted. Their recollections are supported by the compelling fact that the syndicate's eventual involvement in narcotics was a business decision by Luciano that could not have been implemented without the full cooperation of the Buffalo Don, whose territory sat squarely astride the principal narcotics pipeline into the country in the 40's, 50's, and thru the mid 60's.

"brothers George and Elias Eliopoulos": Chandler, at 211-212.

"The Corsican boss": Chandler, at 221-222.

"Magaddino eyed Luciano": anecdotal reconstruction by author based on sources as above.

"Stephano Magaddino was not": Aloi/Don; Camarrata recollections. Camarrata stated to Lanovara that the Don "used to meet with the big boss in Quebec".

"Giuseppe Tangone": a pseudonym used to protect a confidential source. (hereinafter "Tangone")

"Magaddino took Tango at his word": Tango was the Don's man in Montreal.

Chapter 10: Luciano Runs Out of Luck,
The Mob Turns West and Murder, Inc. (pgs. 112-125)

"While Schultz awaited trial": Hammer, at 157-59.

"Dutch Schultz had to go": Hammer, at 162-63, and Sifakis/Mafia, at 297.

"some of the girls to testify": Hammer, at 169; and Messick and Gold-blatt, at 138.

"Magaddino invited his brother-in-law": Lanovara recollections; Tangone recollections.

"The Whiting Avenue neighborhood": the death of Magaddino's sister in the bombing incident is detailed in the archives of both the Buffalo Courier Express and Evening News. Sifakis, himself a former crime reporter in Buffalo, mentions the incident in The Mafia Encyclopedia at. 211. The bombing is usually laid at the doorstep of the Don's brother-in-law, Nick Longo, who is said to have welched on a gambling debt. It may be, however, that Magaddino himself was the target by reason of the apparent betrayal of certain elements of the IRA, who controlled the Montreal docks as the quid pro quo exacted by Provincial police for looking the other way concerning the Don's smuggling activities.

"Lucky Luciano's trial": Sciacca, at 154-65; Luciano's personal recollection of the trial is contained in Martin A. Gosch, and Richard Hammer's, The Last Testament of Lucky Luciano 1974, a work that fell into disrepute when Gosch who allegedly had obtained Luciano's confidence and co-operation and taped his reminiscences, was unable to produce the tapes for review. Carl Sifakis indicates that there may never have been tapes at all, but rather Gosch's largely unintelligible handwritten notes, a circumstance which in and of itself does not label the Luciano "Testament" a literary hoax. The Luciano "Testament" is hereinafter cited Gosch/Hammer.

"Frank Costello acted as a kind of 'prime minister'": Costello's long time friend and attorney, George Wolf, wrote a biography of Costello, Frank Costello Prime Minister of the Underworld. William Morrow & Company, Inc. 1974, with Joseph DiMona (hereinafter "Wolf and DiMona") Costello's personal recollections scheduled for publication in 1975 were cut short by his death.

"Siegel had been in Hollywood": Dean Southern Jennings, We Only Kill Each Other, Prentice-Hall, Inc. 1967 (hereinafter "Jennings") remains the most factual account of the life and bad times of Bugsy Siegel.

"Raft got wind of the plot": Hammer, at 140-42; Jennings,

"In 1937, Vit,o Genovese": the basic reference for material on Don Vitone is the Don Frasca biography, Vito Genovese: King of Crime 1963 (hereinafter "Frasca")

"Count Galeazzo Ciano": Hammer, at 212.

"Carlo Tresca was shot": Hammer at 212. Gage, at 101, posits the theory that Carmine Galante actually pulled the trigger on Tresca.

"Costello wasn't persuaded": Sciacca, at 172.

"The fall of Louis 'Lepke' Buchalter": Lepke's evil genius and down-fall is chronicled in Albert Fried, The Rise and Fall of the Jewish Gangster In America Holt, Rinehart and Winston 1980, at 190-222. (hereinafter "Fried")

"Burton Turkus": Lepke is also the subject of prosecutor Turkus' Mur-der, Inc. Bantam 1960, with Sid Feder. (hereinafter "Turkus")

"It was a sultry summer": Powers/Hoover, at 203.

"Abe Relas, the songbird": Turkus, at 380-81.

Chapter 11: The Flamingo Deal And Luciano's Pardon
Then Havana and Bugsy Siegel (pgs. 126-141)

"Bugsy Siegel gave a glowing": the Polo Grounds meeting to cut up points in the Flamingo is an anecdotal reconstruction by the au-thor based upon disclosures to Babe 'M' during World War II by a pal who was dating Meyer Lansky's daughter, an indiscretion which later cost him his life.

"Joe Zox mentioned to Frank Costello": Charley Lucky's activities on behalf of the allies during the invasion of Sicily is the subject matter of Rod-ney Campbell, The Luciano Project, McGraw-Hill 1977, bibliography at 291 -293. (hereinafter "Campbell")

"The S.S. Normandie had been the pride": Hammer, at 204. and Dennis Eisenberg, Uri Dan, Eli Landau, Meyer Lansky, Mogul of the Mob, Paddington Press Ltd. 1979, 199-204 (hereinafter "Eisenberg/Dan/Landau")

"Messages were delivered by Magaddino": recollections of Spike Lanovara.

"Don Calo Vizzini": Chandler, at 58-61.

"'Operation Underworld'": Campbell, at Messick and Goldblatt, at 157-158.

"the original 'Luciano' signal flag": Chandler, at 58-61; Sciacca, at 184.

"There was a scare in 1944": Hammer, at 210.

"a Petition for Executive Clemency": Hammer, at 210.

"they were greeted by lines of longshoremen": Hammer, at 212; Sciacca, at 188.

"Luciano thanked Don Calo": Sciacca, at 190.

"Interpreter for Colonel Charles Poletti": Sciacca, at 200.

"Lucky Luciano set sail for Havana": Gosch and Hammer, at 106.

"Yet the Flamingo continued to flounder": Jennings, at 152-53, Ed Reid and Ovid Demaris, The Green Felt Jungle, Trident Press 1963, at 24-26 (hereinafter "Reid and Demaris")

"But for Siegel, there": Gosch and Hammer, at 315-316.

"Ruark quickly stumbled": Kitty Kelley, His Way, The Unauthorized Biography of Frank Sinatra, Bantam 1986, at 123. (hereinafter "Kelley")

"Luciano was inclined to give Siegel": Eisenberg, Dan, Landau, at 236. Sciacca paints a somewhat different picture at 197. According to Sciacca, Siegel was immediately marked for death, Lansky's intervention to the contrary notwithstanding. Costello was spared on condition that he personally see to it that the money Siegel skimmed was repaid to his partners, and until Costello made good, he was to step down as Luciano's stateside representative in favor of Vito Genovese.

"Luciano began with a torrent of negatives": Sifakis/Mafia, at 150; and Sciacca, 202-203.

"The Flamingo did reopen": Most of the books previously cited, principally Jennings, Hammer, Eisenberg/Dan/Landau, and Sciacca cover in some detail the "end" of Bugsy Siegel. For reports of Siegel's halcyon days in Vegas and his unexpected demise in Beverly Hills contemporaneous with the events, see the May 27, 1947 issue of Life, at 99, and following, and the July 7, 1947 issue, at 71 and following. The May 27 issue states that visitors to Vegas "can trample the plush carpets at Siegel's $6 million Flamingo Hotel . . . . or perhaps see Frank Sinatra breaking ground for his luxurious new hotel." Strangely, Sinatra's rumored connections to the mob included both Luciano in Havana and his nemesis in Vegas, Bugsy Siegel. Perhaps the most quotable quote of them all appeared at page 73 of the July 7 issue of Life: "Last week a baffled district attorney's investigator said, "Everybody I talked to said they loved the guy."

"The newspaper Siegel had never read": Jennings, at 202-204.

Chapter 12: The Kefauver Hearings and Frank Costello (pgs. 142-150)

"It, was Lansky who enticed Howard Hughes": Sifakis/Mafia, at 160-161.

"the 'pipeline' brought in Number Four": Aloi/Don,

"Magaddino had pioneered mob": Sifakis/Mafia at 211-212.

"Estes Kefauver attended the meetings": Hammer, at 233.

"The Hearings lasted sixteen months": Congressional Record, 1950, 1951.

"There were few answers": Hammer, at 244-51.

"First, he moved against": Hammer, at 259.

"Joe Adonis, another Luciano loyalist": Hammer, at 256-58.

"With their backing and the threat": Bonanno, at. 172-173.

"First, Bonanno began infiltration of": Bonanno himself details his odyssey in <u>A Man of Honor</u> Gay Talese, in <u>Honor Thy Father</u> Fawcett Crest 1971, covers the same ground using personal investigation, principally the disclosures of Bill Bonanno some 14 years before the elder Bonanno chose to speak on the matter. (hereinafter "Talese")

"Bonanno's tentacles reached": Tony Scaduto, The Real Godfather in Penthouse at   (hereinafter "Scaduto")

"Frank Valenti was characterized": Aloi, <u>The Hammer Conspiracies</u> 20th Century Books/Parthenon 1982, at (herein after "Aloi/ Hammer")

"Angelo Acquisto, Magaddino's 'underboss'": Aloi/Don,

"Frank Costello got wind": Bonanno, at 176-181.

189

Chapter 13: Vito Genovese and
Albert the Executioner, Then Apalachin (pgs. 151-165)

"Anastasia and Genovese did just that": Bonanno, at 185.

"'This will go to his head'": Talese, at 34.
"Frank Costello walked out of prison": Wolf and Dimona, at; and Hammer, at 262.

"Costello excused himself": Hammer, at 263-64.

"Gigante, the fat man": Sifakis/Mafia, at 140-141.

"'Gross Casino win - $651,284'": Hammer, at 284.

"Genovese struck first": Hammer, at 269.

"Anastasia elected to muscle": Hammer, at 270-271; Messick and Goldblatt, at 174. Sciacca places a somewhat different reading on Anastasia's alleged move to muscle in on Lansky's Caribbean operations, at 215.

"Genovese gave the Anastasia contract": Sifakis/Mafia, at 130.

"The exiled Lucky Luciano": Sciacca, at 216-217.

"The Jones caper": William Brashier, The Don, The Life and Death of Sam Giancana Harper and Row, 1977, at 101-108.   (hereinafter "Brashler")

"Dio's move was": Sifakis/MaCia, at 109; and Dan F. Moldea, The Hoffa Wars Paddington Press, Ltd. 1978, at 73-75. (hereinafter "Moldea")126.

"Genovese consented, and Bonanno": Bonanno, at 210-215.

"Joseph Bonanno and John Bonventre": Ralph Blumenthal, Last Days of the Sicilians Times Books, 1958, at 51. (hereinafter "Blumenthal") Bonanno's account at 196-201 of his 1957 visit to the old country reads like a travel article for the Guide Michelin and leaves out the Luciano, Bonventre, Galante meeting.

"Bonanno and Magaddino talked": Bonanno, at 212-215.

"The mob's Apalachin fiasco": All of the principal treatments, Hammer, Sifakis, and Messick and Goldblatt have extended treatments of the Apalachin conclave, its causes, and repercussions. So too does Peter Maas, The Valachi Papers Pocket Books 1986, at 208-213. (hereinafter "Maas") The thirtieth anniversary of the mob meeting brought forth a barrage of reminiscences, including those of Trooper Croswell published in the Rochester

Democrat and Chronicle and Times Union, which are included in the author's treatment of the subject.

"Montana explained his 'whereabouts'": Aloi/Don

"Frank Valenti appeared": Aloi/Don, at Aloi/Hammer,

"Someone apparently feared": Sifakis/Mafia, at 211.

"It was all for naught though": Had Magaddino not been a respected mob elder, he certainly would have paid the ultimate penalty for his gaff in insisting that the mob conclave be held in upstate New York. Kobler, at 362.

Chapter 14: The Downfall of Vito Genovese
The Coming of the Kennedys, and Cuba (pgs. 166-174)

"Quickly he targeted Jimmy Hoffa": Steven Brill, The Teamsters Simon and Schuster 1978, at 26-32. (hereinafter "Brill")

"disclosures of Nicola Gentile": some have made the argument that Joe Valachi, concededly only a driver and mob hanger-on, could not have sat in the conclaves of mafia Dons that comprised much of the subject matter of his "papers". It is possible that the FBI used the statements of Gentile, a bonafide mafia Don, to program Valachi. Hammer, at 301-302.

"Joe Kennedy's extra curricular activities": Hammer, at 303-304. Doris Kearns Goodwin in her acclaimed family Kennedy biography, The Fitzgeralds and the Kennedys, Simon and Schuster, 1987, (hereinafter "Kearns") details the Joe Kennedy/Gloria Swanson liaison at 381 and following. She concedes Joe Kennedy's "rumrunning" at 443, but doubts it went so far as to include a partnership with Frank Costello. Costello himself confided in his attorney George Wolf, and author Peter Maas, that he and Joe Kennedy indeed had worked together during Prohibition. John H. Davis, in his The Kennedys, Dynasty and Disaster 1848-1984, McGraw-Hill 1984, at 57 states that in all probability Costello was telling the truth. There simply was no other plausible explanation for the fortune that Joe Kennedy mysteriously amassed during Prohibition. (hereinafter "Davis/ Dynasty")

"the 'garrote' murder of her lover, Steve Franse": Hammer, at 275-76.

"Nelson Cantellops delivered a bravura": Hammer, at 277. Sifakis/ Mafia, at 138. Both Hammer and Sifakis question the bona fides of Cantellops' revelations. Eisenberg, Dan and Landau, the biographers of Meyer Lansky, flat out state at 248-249 that Genovese's downfall at the hands of Cantellops was the handiwork of Meyer Lansky.

"Racetracks were Bufalino's specialty": Aloi/Don. Original research by author in archives of Binghamton newspapers which compiled over the years and maintain an extensive file on Russell Bufalino that includes reports and articles, as well as materials from law enforcement sources. Bufalino also is the subject of an extensive background file in the archives of the Buffalo Evening News.

"It was Roselli who engineered": G. Robert Blakey and Richard N. Billings, The Plot To Kill the President, Times Books 1981, at 383- 389. (hereinafter "Blakey")

"the radio blared out news of Raul Castro": Trumbull Higgins, The Perfect Failure: Kennedy Eisenhower and the CIA at the Bay of Pigs, Norton 1987, bibliography 207-219. (hereinafter "Higgins")

"and branded an undesirable alien": Aloi/Don,

"Ambassador Earl E.T. Smith reported to President Eisenhower": Philip W. Bonsal, Cuba Castro, and the United States University of Pittsburg Press 1971, at 171 (hereinafter "Bonsal")

"Trafficante was languishing in a Cuban prison": Henry Hurt, Reasonable Doubt, An Investigation Into The Assassination of John F. Kennedy Henry Holt and Company 1985, at, 178-179 (hereinafter "Hurt"); and Blakey, at 293.

"Fidel Castro was not a communist": Wayne S. Smith, The Closest of Enemies W.W. Norton and Company 1987, at 44 (hereinafter "Smith")

"Ruby played middle man": Blakey, at 293.

"a French freighter loaded with": Bonsal treats the sinking of the La Coubre at 133 and following.

BIBLIOGRAPHY

Additional source material for the Gangster Chronicles, and reader's interested in a deeper dive into the murky depths of organized crime in America, follows:

Dary Matera, John Dillinger: The Life and Death of America's First Celebrity Criminal, Da Capo Press (2004).

Bryan Burrough, Public Enemies: American's Greatest Crime Wave and the Birth of the FBI 1933-34, Penguin Books, (2004) and (2005).

Luciano Iorizzo, Al Capone: A Biography, Greenwood Press (2003).

Selwyn Raab, Five Families: The Rise, Decline, and Resurgence of America's Most Powerful Mafia Empires, Thomas Dunne Books (2005).

Charles River Editors, Bugsy Siegel and Meyer Lansky: The Controversial Mobsters Who Worked With Lucky Luciano to Form the National Crime Syndicate, Create Space Publishing (2018).

Bradley Lewis: Hollywood's Celebrity Gangsters: The Incredible Life and Times of Mickey Cohen, BBL Books (2009).

Bradley Lewis, Mickey Cohen: The Rat Pack Years: the Elder Statesman's Life and Times, 1960-1976, BBL Books (2014).

James Banks, Frank Sinatra: The Dark Story of His Mafia Connection (2015).

Hickman Powell, Lucky Luciano: The Man Who Organized Crime in America, Barricade Books, Incorporated, (2004) and (2015).

Michael Newton, Boss of Murder, Inc. The Criminal Life of Albert Anastasia, Exposit Books (2020).

Lee Server, Handsome Johnny: The Life and Death of Johnny Rosselli: Gentleman Gangster, Hollywood Producer, and CIA Assassin, St. Martin's Press (2018).

Leonard Katz, Uncle Frank: The Biography of Frank Costello, Drake Publisher (1973).

Dennis Eisenberg, Meyer Lansky, Mogul of the Mob, Paddington Press (1979).

Anthony M. DeStefano, Top Hoodlum: Frank Costello, Prime Minister of the Mafia, Citadel (2018).

Al Moe, Vegas and the Mob: Forty Years of Frenzy, Amazon.com Services LLC (2013).

Michael Newton, Mr. Mob: The Life and Crimes of Moe Dalitz, McFarland (2009).

Vincent Patrick, Goodbye Fella's (2007).

Allan R. May, Gangland Gotham: New York's Notorious Mob Bosses, Greenwood (2009).

James B. Jacobs, Mobsters, Unions, and Feds: The Mafia and the American Labor Movement, New York University Press (2006).

James B. Jacobs, Coleen Friel, Robert Radick, Gotham Unbound: How New York City Was Liberated From the Grip of Organized Crime, New York University Press (1999).

Marc Mappen, Prohibition Gangsters: The Rise and Fall of a Bad Generation, Rutgers University Press (2013).

David E. Kaplan, Alec Dubro, Yakuza: Japan's Criminal Underworld, University of California Press (2012).

Peter B. E. Hill, The Japanese Mafia: Yakuza, Law, and the State, Oxford University Press (2003).

Lee Bernstein, The Greatest Menace: Organized Crime in Cold

War America, University of Massachusetts Press (2002).

Federico Varese, The Russian Mafia: Private Protection in a New Market Economy, Oxford University Press (2001).

Robert J. Kelly, Encyclopedia of Organized Crime in the United States: From Capone's Chicago to the New Urban Underworld, Greenwood Press (2000).

Gus Russo, The Outfit: The Role of Chicago's Underworld in the Shaping of Modern America, Bloomberg (2003).

Dan Herbeck, The Mafia is all but Dead in Western New York. So What Killed It? The Buffalo Evening News article, March 19, 20, 2017.

Mike Hudson, Mob May Be Dead But Not Forgotten, Niagara Falls Reporter, Sept. 18, 2012.

Picture Footnotes:

Benito Mussolini pg. 10 https://allthatsinteresting.com/benito-mussolini-death (photo)
Cascio Ferro pg.12 Photo from Wikipedia
Cesare Mori pg.14 Wikipedia
Stephano Magaddino pg. 15 Wikipedia
Antonino "Nino" Magaddino pg. 16 http:/buffalomob.blogspot.com/2013/09/antonino-magaddino-june-18-1897-to.html (photo)
Joseph Bonanno pg. 17 https://www.findagrave.com/memorial/6454548/joseph-bonanno
Gasper Milazzo pg. 17 https://www.findagrave.com/memorial/6284807/gasper-milazzo
Salvatore Maranzano pg.18 https://allthatsinteresting.com/salvatore-maranzano
Meeting of the Mafia at Cleveland's Hotel Statler. Pg.19 https:shekoos.wordpress.com/2011/05/31/mafia-at-clevelands-hotel-statler/ "1928 Mafia Convention Picture"
Joe Masseria pg. 20 Wikipedia
Al Capone and St. Valentine's Day Massacre pg. 21 https://www.britannica.com/biography/Al-Capone (photo)
Charles "Lucky" Luciano pg.23 Wikipedia
Joe Aiello pg.24 https://www.pinterest.com/pin/377669118729019764/
Joe Valachi pg. 24 Wikipedia
Frank Costello pg. 19 https://www.crimemuseum.org/crime-library/organized-crime/frank-costello/
Joe "the Boss" Masseria dead pg. 26 https://allthatsinteresting.com/joe-masseria
Vincent "Mad Dog" Coll pg. 28 Wikipedia
Salvatore Maranzano dead pg. 29 http://gangstersinc.ning.com/profiles/blogs/american-mafia-s-boss-of-bosses-whacked-at-his-office
Bugsy Siegel pg. 30 https://www.britannica.com/biography/Bugsy-Siegel
Joe Bonanno pg. 30 Wikipedia
Mafia Commission in 1931 pg.31 https://mafiagame.fandom.com/wiki/The_Commission
Albert Anastasia pg. 31 https://themobmuseum.org/notable_names/albert-anastasia/
Lepke Buchalter pg. 31 https://americanmafiahistory.com/louis-lepke-buchalter/
Capone Guilty newspaper pg. 33 https://www.mightytaxes.com/al-capone-tax-evasion/
Jake Lingle pg.34 https://en.wikipedia.org/wiki/Jake_Lingle
Anton Cermak pg. 41 https://www.britannica.com/biography/Anton-J-Cermak

Frank Nitti pg. 42 Wikipedia

Harry Pierpont pg. 44 http://www.executedtoday.com/tag/harry-pierpont

Johnny Dillinger pg. 44 https://www.fbi.gov/history/famous-cases/john-dillinger

Jack McGurn pg. 46 https://www.babyfacenelsonjournal.com/jack-mcgurn.html

Anton Cermak pg. 47 https://www.britannica.com/biography/Anton-J-Cermak

Joseph Zangara pg. 49 https://en.wikipedia.org/wiki/Giuseppe_Zangara

Biograph Theatre pg. 52 http://cinematreasures.org/theaters/273

Louis Piquett pg.56 http://star-spangled.narod.ru/gang/johndill.htm

Frank 'Jelly' Nash pg. 57 pinterest.com

Willie Bioff pg. 61 https://babbittblog.com/2016/10/09/disney-and-the-mob-willie-bioff/

Harry Pierpont pg. 63 Wikipedia

Louis Piquett pg. 72

Lester Gillis aka Baby Face Nelson pg. 74 https://www.fbi.gov/history/famous-cases/lester-gillis-baby-face-nelson

Bonnie and Clyde death car pg. 84 https://www.birthfactdeathcalendar.net/events/23-may-1934-b/

Biograph Theatre Pg. 92 https://people.howstuffworks.com/john-dillinger.htm

John Dillinger dead pg. 94 https://apnews.com/ "Dillinger relatives doubt body in grave is the gangster" By Rick Callahan Aug. 1, 2019

Melvin Purvis pg. 100 Wikipedia

Frank Nitti dead pg. 101 https://www.nationalcrimesyndicate.com/frank-nitti-death-photos/

Willie Bioff's car pg. 102 https://www.facebook.com/valleyrelics/photos/&theater

Stephano Magaddino pg. 106 https://buffalonews.com/2017/03/19/fbi-says-buffalos-mafia-family-ceased-operations/

Dutch Schultz pg. 113 Wikipedia

Dutch Schultz death scene pg. 115 https://www.nationalcrimesyndicate.com/dutch-schultz-death-scene-photos/

Tom Dewey pg. 116 https://www.britannica.com/biography/Thomas-E-Dewey

Niagara Falls Gazette newspaper pg. 119 "Bombing Kills Woman Here"

Vito Genovese pg.121 https://themobmuseum.org/notable_names/vito-genovese/

Frank Costello pg. 123 https://themobmuseum.org/notable_names/frank-costello/

Abe Relas body pg. 125 http://archive.boxing.media/hard_jews.html "Abe Relas dead"

Charles "Lucky" Luciano deported pg. 132 http://www.apimages.com/metadata/Index/Associated-Press-Domestic-News-New-York-United-/deb10e4d9ae5da11af9f0014c2589dfb "Luciano Deported"

Fulgencio Batista, Thelma Lansky, Meyer Lansky pg. 134 https://www.wikiwand.com/en/Hotel_Nacional_de_Cuba

Sinatra and the mob in Havana, 1946 pg. 135 https://www.sandiegoreader.com/news/2016/mar/21/ticker-cuba-mafia-sinatra-smith-and-penasquitos/# "Havana Convention photo with Sinatra"

Bugsy Siegel mug shot pg. 136 https://themobmuseum.org/notable_names/benjamin-bugsy-siegel/

Flamingo Hotel pg. 140 http://blog.caesars.com/las-vegas/las-vegas-hotels/flamingo-las-vegas-70-anniversary/

Bugsy Siegel dead pg. 141 https://www.anacortesgunshop.com/the-glamorous-life-and-gory-death-of-the-father-of-sin-city-bugsy-siegel-the-m1-carbine-and-murder-inc

Senator Kefauver pg. 145 https://www.senate.gov/artandhistory/history/common/image/KefauverCommittee_microphone.htm

Frank Costello pg. 146 https://commons.wikimedia.org/wiki/File:Frank_Costello_-_Kefauver_Committee.jpg

Frank Costello testifying pg. 147 https://justcriminals.info/2016/11/12/frank-costello-1952/

Willie Moretti dead pg. 148 http://gangstersinc.ning.com/photo/1951-murder-of-willie-moretti

Frank Valenti pg. 149 https://mafia.wikia.org/wiki/Frank_Valenti

Vito Genovese pg. 152 https://themobmuseum.org/notable_names/vito-genovese/

Albert Anastasia pg.152 https://themobmuseum.org/notable_names/albert-anastasia/

Vincent "The Chin" Gigante pg. 154 https://en.wikipedia.org/wiki/Vincent_Gigante

Crazy Joe Gallo pg. 155 https://www.ebay.com/itm/CRAZY-JOE-GALLO-8X10-PHOTO-MAFIA-ORGANIZED-CRIME-MOBSTER-MOB-PICTURE-/333152207159

Albert Anastasia dead pg. 156 http://joegiacalone.net/mobs-greatest-unsolved-hits-albert-anastasia/

Sam Giancana pg. 157 https://www.biography.com/crime-figure/Sam Giancana

Joe Barbara's 130 acre estate pg. 160 https://www.democratandchronicle.com/story/news/2019/02/07/rochester-mafia-mystery-jake-russo-killed-pizza-stop-basement-frank-valenti-apalachin-meeting/2191800002/ "Photo of Barbara's House"

John C. Montana pg. 163 http://buffalomob.blogspot.com/2013/09/john-montana-july-1-1893-march-18-1964.html

Frank Valenti (left) and Stan Valenti pg. 165 Wikipedia, Pinterest

J. Edgar Hoover pg. 167 https://www.britannica.com/biography/J-Edgar-Hoover

Joe Kennedy pg. 168 Wikipedia

Anna and Vito Genovese pg. 169 Pinterest.com

John Roselli pg. 171 http://mafiasome.blogspot.com/2017/02/john-roselli.html

Russell J. Bufalino and Thomas Lucchese pg. 172 https://www.timesleader.com/news/751375/profiling-the-low-profile-godfather-russell-bufalino "Photo of Bufalino and Luchese testifying."

Santos Trafficante pg. 173 https:mafia.wikia.org/wiki Santo Trafficante, Jr.

Other books by the authors:

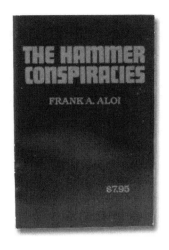

"The Hammer Conspiracies"

By Frank A. Aloi

© 1982

"The Hammer Conspiracies" details investigations of Mafia activity in Rochester, N. Y., the subsequent trials, and the debacle that followed. It is a story of perjured detectives, gang wars, organized crime, overthrown convictions, imprisoned law enforcement officers and prosecutors, faulty police work, and corrupt officials.

Vincent "Jimmy the Hammer" Massaro was hit by the mob. His death generated conspiracy prosecutions against what was alleged to be the top echelon of the organization in Rochester, N. Y. The testimony of informers, including two of the alleged triggermen, and detectives who surveilled mob meetings where Massaro's fate was plotted, produced convictions. But there had been no surveillances. Detectives admitted perjuring themselves. Alleged mobsters were released from prison. A bloody gang war erupted, and Federal Indictments were returned against Detectives and Prosecutors. A saga of fabricated evidence and corruption unprecedented in the war against organized crime.

Other books by the authors:

"The Rochester Mob Wars"

By Blair T. Kenny

© 2017

"The Rochester Mob Wars" is the true story about the rise and fall of the Rochester Mafia. The Rochester Mafia Crime Family boasted over 40 "made" members in its heyday, before internal strife and power struggles led to its demise by self destruction via murder, shootings, and bombings.

"The Rochester Mob Wars" book is the result of two years of research into organized crime in Rochester, N. Y. The book is a compilation of newspaper clippings, court documents, and Senate Hearings placed in chronological order detailing the highlights of the Mob's activity over a 40 year period. The 208 page book covers the time period of the 1950's to 1997 when Teamsters Local #398 was put into "Trusteeship" for lifetime affiliation with the Mafia.

Other books by the authors:

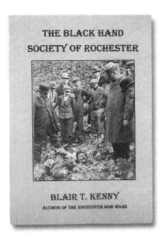

"The Black Hand Society of Rochester"

By Blair T. Kenny

© 2019

"The Black Hand Society of Rochester" is the prequel to "The Rochester Mob Wars." Beginning with Italian Immigration, the 342 page book uncovers the origins of the Rochester Mafia, which had its roots in the Italian Camorra and their American branch called "The Black Hand". In similar fashion to the Mob Wars book, "The Black Hand Society of Rochester" documents organized criminal activities of Rochester mobsters from 1900-1948. The book comes complete with an index of more than 600 names and eight pages of mobster profiles.

therochestermobwars.com

Other books by the authors:

"Enter The C-Team"

By Blair T. Kenny and Frank A. Aloi

Narrated by Thomas Taylor

© 2020

"Enter The C-Team" offers a rare glimpse into the interworking's of the Rochester Mafia as seen through the eyes of Thomas Taylor; friend, driver and bodyguard for Rochester Mafia Underboss Sammy "G" Gingello. Taylor, a former A-Team member gives a first hand account of fighting on both the A-Team and the C-Team, the third faction in Rochester's Mafia Alphabet Wars. It is a story of bombings, shootings, treachery and murder highlighting an intense struggle for power. At stake was control of Rochester, N.Y.'s organized Crime Family and all its rackets.

**All Chapter Caricatures and Cover Design
are the original artwork
of Sam Villareale**

**Copyright © 2020
- Sam Villareale -**

Villastrations
Caricatures, Portraits, Pet Portraits, Custom Illustrations

Contact Sam @

http://www.villastrations.com/

A special thank you goes to Wendy Post, Sample Media Group editor and reporter, former Department of Defense News Writer and Army Veteran residing near Apalachin, N.Y. and originally from Rochester, N.Y.